How To Books

Be a Great Salesperson

Be a Great Salesperson

*Powerful techniques to make that
sale and boost your career*

RICHARD HESSION

How To Books

Published by How To Books Ltd,
3 Newtec Place, Magdalen Road,
Oxford OX4 1RE. United Kingdom.
Tel: (01865) 793806. Fax: (01865) 248780.
email: info@howtobooks.co.uk
www.howtobooks.co.uk

British Library Cataloguing in Publication Data
A catalogue record for this book is available from the British
Library.

Edited by David Kershaw
Cartoons by Mike Flanagan
Cover design by Shireen Nathoo Design
Cover image PhotoDisc
Cover copy by Sallyann Sheridan

Produced for How To Books by Deer Park Productions
Typeset by Anneset, Weston-super-Mare, Somerset
Printed and bound by Cromwell Press, Trowbridge, Wiltshire

NOTE: The material contained in this book is set out in good
faith for general guidance and no liability can be accepted for
loss or expense incurred as a result of relying in particular
circumstances on statements made in the book. Laws and
regulations are complex and liable to change, and readers
should check the current position with the relevant authori-
ties before making personal arrangements.

Contents

List of Illustrations

Preface

By choosing selling as a career, you have entered a profession that not only promises good rewards but, most importantly, gives you job satisfaction – something sadly a lot of people never get to experience during the whole of their working lives.

Ask any successful salesperson and they'll tell you that selling is – and should be above everything else – fun. You're lucky to be in such a pleasurable occupation that lets your personal enjoyment and enthusiasm shine through and inspire others. And there is nothing like the buzz you get each time you win over a customer and close a deal. It's a reward in itself.

As well as being challenging and exhilarating, sales career tests you physically and mentally, develops your social skills and helps you realise your true potential as an individual. There are very few professions where each day offers fresh opportunities, brings new faces and places; where you find yourself taken through the whole range of human emotions and gain a real zest for living.

Our society owes its prosperity to good salesmanship. The whole economic process depends on the salesperson setting the wheels in motion. Just as great oaks begin as little acorns, so all great things start with an idea. Basically, selling is motivating your fellow men and women through ideas – stimulating and encouraging them to think for themselves and helping them make the right choices that will create prosperity for their organisations and ultimately enrich their lives.

Selling is the driving force behind Business. However sound the financial investment, efficient the manufacturing production process and excellent the finished product, nothing can happen until the salesperson at the sharp end puts the wheels in motion. Everything ultimately depends on your efforts and imaginative creativity in formulating the ideas to generate sales.

Always remember it is a great privilege to be a salesperson. With that privilege comes responsibility. You belong to that sector of commercial activity in which you – and you alone – can determine the level of success to which you aspire. Dedication to your profession, coupled with the skills you will learn here, will enable you to achieve that goal.

Successful selling!

Richard Hession

Acknowledgements

Grateful thanks must go to all those who have exerted influence in my sales life – too numerous to mention here. They run from my various mentors in the companies for whom I have been fortunate to work, through to the professional trainers and coaches who have made such a positive impact in improving my sales results.

1

Prospecting

KEEPING YOUR ATTENTION ON THE THREE BASIC STEPS

As far as getting new customers is concerned, there are three, basically simple, steps in the total selling process:

1. Find your prospects.
2. Make your presentations.
3. Achieve the sales.

Everything you plan and do must contribute something to one of these steps.

As you gain in experience and your selling skills develop, keep a critical eye on your technique and the systems you employ. If anything stands in the way of your achieving the three basic steps, modify, change or dispose of it altogether.

DON'T BECOME A PAPER SHUFFLER

It's all too easy to become a paper shuffler or a systems fanatic. Some salespeople produce sales reports, graphs and analyses of buying trends without getting round to actually selling! This doesn't mean to say that a systematic approach to selling isn't important, or that report writing isn't needed. You have to maintain records and deal with a certain amount of paperwork, but this is a means to an end, not the end itself. It is part of self-management and required by other members of the sales team.

FINDING PROSPECTIVE CUSTOMERS

There are standard techniques for obtaining leads and we'll be looking at these. But before doing that, let's talk about prospective customers. How can we tell if someone is a good prospect? Most people will most likely express interest, but you have to identify those among them who will really benefit from your product or service. There are three essential qualifications a genuine prospective customer must possess:

- **M**oney to spend
- **A**uthority to pay
- A real **N**eed

summed up by the mnemonic **MAN**.

As a professional salesperson you should aim to line up a number of prospects who appear to fit the bill and to which you can add, so that you always have a progression of prospective buyers (Figure 1):

- At the start of the line-up will be *new* prospects, ones who appear to have the potential but require further investigation.
- Next come the *qualified* ones – those with MAN (money, authority and need).
- They're followed by *hot prospects*, who are the buyers to whom you're selling now, particularly where the closing stage has been reached.
- Last, but certainly not least, are *re-established* prospects. They're the people who, when originally approached, didn't have a need for your product or service at that time. Since then, however, perhaps circumstances have changed and a need might well have developed.

Remember, keeping up a flow through all four stages will ensure prospecting success.

PROSPECTING TECHNIQUES

Now, as promised, are ways of finding prospective customers that prove successful.

By telephone

Cold calling by telephone is one of the most useful methods of canvassing. It gives good results, but is only really successful if you can project your enthusiasm over the line. A telephone call enables you fairly quickly to

- sound out the people you talk to
- establish if they fulfil the MAN principle and, if so
- introduce your organisation and sell your product or service.

There are certain psychological advantages, too – you gain prestige when fixing an appointment, because you're calling at the prospect's invitation. Telephone canvassing also allows you to plan your selling time and sales call.

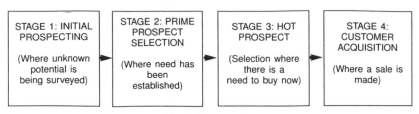

Fig. 1. Prospecting.

Eye balling

This method of prospecting is a variation of telephone canvassing. It involves selecting an area and, street by street, listing likely companies which are then telephoned. As well as having the advantages of telephone selling, it groups calls in one geographical area and gives you, the salesperson, familiarity with the area and the companies you are targeting.

Cold canvassing

A convenient way to seek out prospects, cold canvassing is virtually venturing into the unknown by knocking on the doors of companies who may or may not be qualified. Right from the start, it's vital to find out if the person receiving you has MAN and your sales pitch is going to lead into the sale. Cold canvassers build up their own repertoire of opening phrases, questions and follow-ons to get this information quickly.

Recommendation

If you're a good salesperson, you'll find that satisfied customers will create opportunities by referring others to you. Recommendation by word of mouth is one of the best forms of introduction to new prospects who will be already partly sold on the idea.

Clubs and societies

Accepting an invitation to become a Rotarian or Round Tabler, or in the case of a saleswoman membership of a professional or business women's club, has advantages. So does joining a local Chamber of Commerce. It enables you to meet people of influence in business or community circles. Similarly quite a lot of business is done on the golf course!

Radiation

This involves asking a prospective customer for the names of other potential clients. You can broach the subject during the presentation or after closing successfully.

General observation

There are always plenty of leads to follow if you use your eyes and wits. Read newspapers, magazines, trade journals and business directories. Newspaper and magazine advertisements are a particularly rich source of information. Scan the tenders and contracts columns and don't forget the posts vacant section – a company advertising for personnel is probably embarking on an expansion programme. Local *Thomson Directories* and *Yellow Pages* will also 'let your fingers do the walking'.

Records

Many companies will sell information to salespeople in the form of card systems or computer printouts listing the names of various companies. Again, don't forget your own company's records. Existing customers could well be persuaded to make even more use of your product or service. Look through your old sales reports and those of other salespeople who might have covered your territory before you. It's worth approaching former customers to find out why they no longer avail themselves of your company's services and to bring them up to date with recent developments.

Prospect spotters

In some instances, outside people seek out prospective buyers and pass details on to the sales team. They are normally paid a commission at the conclusion of a successful sale.

Co-operation

It's worth talking with other salespeople who, although they call on the same kind of customer as you, have a product or service not in competition with yours.

Company backing

You'll be responsible for initiating the canvassing techniques described so far, but your own company can assist you find prospects by creating response from advertising campaigns, special sales events, trade displays and stands at national exhibitions.

TO SUM UP

Find your prospective customers – remember the mnemonic **MAN**. Keeping a flow through all the four stages of the prospecting procedure will ensure success. Use all the ways of finding prospective customers you can think of.

2

Appointments by Phone

MAKING FRIENDS WITH THE TELEPHONE

We tend to take the phone for granted as a familiar form of everyday communication in home and office. But how many salespeople have really given it some thought and taken the trouble to develop the necessary telephonic skills to win them sales? Believe it or not there are still some otherwise good salespeople who fight shy of using the phone. Fear of not saying the right thing or becoming tongue tied causes them to adopt a negative attitude towards phoning for an appointment. Like most things, it's a matter of discipline and preparation. Be confident and your confidence will come over in your voice.

Making appointments by phone is the quickest, cheapest and most efficient method (Figure 2). While there's seldom any difficulty fixing appointments with buyers who have an interest in your product or service, there could be difficulty where no interest exists and has to be created.

CLARIFYING YOUR OBJECTIVES

Before you pick up the phone, first get your objectives clear. You should ask yourself why you're making the call. Now, what are you going to say? If it's to fix an appointment, a call lasting no more than a minute should be sufficient to enable you to say all you want to.

MAKING YOURSELF ATTRACTIVE

The next thing to remember is that you cannot be seen by prospective buyers to whom you're speaking, but they're going to have a mental picture of you based on what they can hear. So you must concentrate on making your voice convey the confidence you feel mixed with

*   enthusiasm
*   maturity
*   a businesslike approach

- warmth – yes!
- and even the suggestion of a friendly smile.

Remember, those who don't ask, don't get. You're going to ask the prospect for an appointment and you're going to expect them to agree to seeing you – so confidently and with minimum delay, launch into the reason for your call.

BEING ALERT TO OBJECTIONS

There are likely to be a few objections on the prospect's part – no one likes to think they're a pushover, particularly to a salesperson – but most of these are predictable and can be dealt with by you. Common ones are along the lines of:

- I'm far too busy to see anyone this week . . .
- I've got to clear things up before I go on holiday . . .
- Drop me a line telling me what you want to talk about . . .
- Send me a brochure . . .
- I'm not ready to talk to any reps about our plans yet . . .

> **Always be ready to anticipate standard objections and spend some time preparing good convincing answers to them.**

BEING BRIEF BUT INTRIGUING

For your part, you must always be ready with a brief, but intriguing, reason why you should meet which will arouse the prospect's interest and curiosity: 'I want to come and discuss with you how to streamline your operation . . .' or 'I want to show you two new developments in your particular field which will give you the edge over competitors . . .' Put yourself in the prospect's place – is the reason good enough to warrant you being granted an appointment by a busy buyer?

CLOSING

Always have your diary ready – and use it verbally to fix a date. Develop the habit of closing your phone conversation gently, politely but positively, making sure you confirm the details of date, time and place. If an appointment can't be fixed there and then, make clear you'll be phoning again – after the prospect's return from holiday, for example.

Now for a look in detail at the technique of successful appointment making by phone.

REMEMBERING YOUR AIMS

- Keep in mind the aim of your call – the appointment.

- Clarify your identify and that of your company, to avoid the risk of not being subsequently recognised on the phone or in person.

- Gain the prospect's attention by introducing facts that show you have done your homework and shown *your* interest in their company.

- Appeal to the buying motives of the prospect, if you know them, or employ something novel in keeping with their current interests.

- Give good, sound reasons why the prospect should see you. Don't, however, be drawn into explanations and prolong the phone call.

- Close on your aim as soon as you can and ask for the appointment. Always give the prospect a choice of two days and suggest times and dates which fit into your own plan.

- Leave the next move up to the prospect. Hard as it may be for you as a salesperson, keep quiet!

NOT LETTING QUESTIONS GET IN THE WAY

Try to avoid questions from the prospect which seeks information until you have achieved your aim of fixing a definite appointment.

If a prospect insists on asking questions, use them to achieve your aim – for example, 'Delivery times depend on a number of factors, including size and quantity. I'll be in a better position to tell you about delivery in more detail when we meet. I could call on you next Thursday, or would Friday suit you better?'

Tips for making successful telephone appointments
- Always refer to a prospect by first name and second name when speaking to switchboard operators or secretaries. This gives the impression you know the prospect well and will ease access to them.

- Always be polite but firm and don't waste your time by being drawn into giving information to people other than the prospect.

- If the prospect is unavailable, find out when they will be available and arrange to call back. Always keep the initiative.

Introduction

Why is it so important?
First impressions
Positive professionalism
What should I say and why?
Think what could be happening at the other
end of the line and give them time to 'tune
in'

Message

What do I want to convey?
Who my company is and what we do
Why? To inform and whet the appetite
How? Concisely and effectively

Purpose

What I want to achieve (an appointment)
How the prospect could benefit
An example of special benefit to the
prospect
Why the prospect should consider *me*
An example of how others have benefited

Action

Ask for the appointment
'So, would you be free for a short time on
. . . or . . . ?'
Deal with any objections
Agree, re-state, reassure

Close

Specify
Offer alternatives, such as a.m. or p.m.

Thank

the prospect positively and sincerely, and
confirm the *day, date, time, place*
'Thank you, so I look forward to meeting
you on Tuesday the 6th at 2 p.m. at your
head office in Chester . . .'
'Thank you again, Mr Jones. Goodbye . . .'

Fig. 2. A guide to telephoning: how to achieve maximum *impact*.

- If you have a third party's name as a reference, always use it – for example, 'Bill Jones suggested I give you a call, Mr Brown, regarding your ideas for refurbishing your company's offices'.

OVERCOMING OBJECTIONS TO APPOINTMENT GETTING

Now let's look more closely at some of the objections likely to be raised and how we're going to overcome them. Imagine the dialogue in your mind and play through it until you're familiar with the general strategy of tackling objections:

- first a with a 'cushion' reply
- then follow-up questions and, where appropriate
- closing with a definite agreed action or alternative choices of date, time and place for meeting.

I've got someone with me, you've caught me in a meeting . . .
Be brief, but to the point with:

- 'Sorry, I'll call you back . . . later today or tomorrow?'
- 'What time do you usually get in?'
- 'I'll talk to your secretary and fix with her a more convenient time to call . . .'

I'm too busy to see you . . .
A good old standard this! The obvious cushion reply from you is:

- 'Sorry to hear that . . .' with a follow-up of:
- 'Perhaps if we could look a little further ahead then . . .'

If the prospect suggests a meeting too far ahead, try this as an alternative close:

- 'Forgive me, but can I just say that I'm a little worried that if we don't meet until then, will I still have the chance to talk to you about . . . ? So, working on that basis, how about . . . ?'

I'm up to my eyes in at the moment – I'll call you back . . .
You know from experience it's unlikely the prospect will get back to you, so:

- 'Thanks. That's very kind of you. However, I'm going to be moving around and I'm not sure when I'll be back in the office. If I may, please, I'd like to call *you* back. When's the best day to talk to you . . . or . . . ? And around what time?'

Send me some literature, like a brochure and price list . . .
The cushion reply is:

- 'I'm sorry, I don't have any literature, as ours is a product/service tailored to the individual needs of your company. It's better if I discuss things with you and show you examples . . . ?' Or follow-ups such as:
- 'When could I bring it around . . . ?'
- 'So, why don't we look at say . . . or . . . ?'
- 'It's difficult answering questions on the phone. I think it better if we meet. How about . . . ?'

Alternative closes could be along the following lines:

- 'Delighted to . . .'
- 'I'll pop it in the post now. Depending on the postal system, you should get it tomorrow.'
- 'I send you what we've got, so that you have Friday (or the week-end) to read it and I'll phone you on Monday . . .'

I've nothing for you at present . . .
Cushion reply:

- 'Sure, I appreciate that . . .' But better is the alternative close:
- 'The reason I'd like to come and see you is to talk about your future needs, rather than your current ones. By talking now, you'll be in the picture regarding the help we can give your company when you're ready . . .'

I'm not ready to discuss things with you . . .
Don't delay. Get in with alternatives at once:

- 'When would be the earliest suitable date – later this week . . . or perhaps next week would be better . . .'
- 'By the way, could I ask how many other companies are likely be asked . . . ?'
- 'What needs to be done between now and the date we've arranged to get together . . . ?'

Depending on the reply, you might find you have to pull back and call back or else go for a date well ahead.

I'm quite happy with the present arrangements . . .

The cushion reply is:

* 'Of course . . .' Try the comparison follow-up:
* 'I'd like to explore with you ways by which we could help develop (or improve) your existing system. You can then at least compare . . .'

Or a combination of the following will still leave the door open:

* 'How often do you carry out a review . . . ?'
* 'When do you review . . . ?'
* 'When does the review period begin . . . ?'
* 'What areas would you like to see some kind of improvement in . . . ?'
* 'What would you do if it wasn't possible to . . . ?'
* 'What would you do then . . . ?'

Your answer to the prospect's replies to any of the above should be: 'So if . . . ?'

You'll need to speak to my assistant/buyer . . .

* 'Thank you – I'll be happy to do so, of course . . .' is the cushion, followed by:
* 'But it was my understanding that I should speak with you . . . is that not correct?'
* 'My reason for asking to talk to you is simply to get your approval of the concept of . . . If you like it, then I'll be delighted to talk it over in more detail with . . .'

Your subsequent question should be:

* 'If I speak to your assistant, do they have the authority to give me the go-ahead . . . ?'

Who told you I'm the one to speak to . . . ?

State the source of your information, then check if it is correct.

We haven't any money . . . ?

The cushion reply is:

* 'I appreciate the problem . . . ?' Subsequent questions are:
* 'When does your next financial year start . . . ?'
* 'When do budgets have to be completed by and when will you know your allocation . . . ?'

Followed by:

- 'So, if we start to talk now . . .'
- 'Tell me, would such an expenditure (or investment) be regarded as capital or revenue . . . ?'
- 'Who else is involved in these decisions . . . ?'

Right, tell me now . . . or Exactly what do you do . . . ?

- 'Delighted to . . .'
- 'My company is . . .'
- 'What particular aspects of . . . are you involved with . . . ?'
- 'How familiar are you with our new . . . ?'

Followed by: 'So if . . . ?'

Why is your company so much better . . . ?

- 'A number of reasons . . . ?' And go on to list them, followed up by:
- 'I'm not saying that we are better than your present supplier. What I am saying is our customers bought our products/services because . . .'

Remember, never bad mouth your competitors – it could backfire!

I already know about your company and what you do . . .

Never take this for granted. Persist with:

- 'Forgive me, but I wasn't aware of that . . .'
- 'Whom did you speak with . . . ?'
- 'Which office . . . ? And when was that . . . ?'
- 'Which of our products/services was it in connection with . . . ?'
- 'How familiar are you with our *new* . . . updated models . . . latest services . . . improved specifications . . . adding value?'
- 'So if . . . ?'

I've had bad experience of your company before . . .

Don't let this objection faze you. Turn it to your advantage with the cushion reply:

- 'I'm sorry to hear that . . . ?' Then investigate the truth of the allegation and show your concern by asking:
- 'What happened . . . ?'
- 'How long ago was that . . . ?'

- 'What was done to correct it . . . . ?'

Now comes the moment to turn an apparent disadvantage to your advantage:

- 'So if I could show you . . . ?'

TO SUM UP

Remember, be positive, not negative. The prospect won't be expecting your call and indeed there's no reason why you should be turned down.

Everything's in your favour as a well trained professional salesperson. You've given a lot of thought to the effective use of the phone and voice technique. You're quite clear on your objectives, thought of all the possible objections that could come your way and have developed good answers to them. Your diary is ready at hand, you're in control of the situation, and you have enthusiasm and belief in your success.

No matter how skilled a salesperson you are, you won't achieve your objective on the phone every time, but at least seven out of ten times you will – with measured thought, planning and practice.

3

Getting to the Decision-maker without an Appointment

When cold calling or dropping in on the spur of the moment, you must ensure you don't waste your time or someone else's by trying to sell to the wrong person – a person who does not have the buying power vested in the true decision-maker.

WHO IS THE RIGHT PERSON?

Earlier on we identified decision-makers as people with, in most cases, the *money*, the *authority* and the *need*, which we can conveniently remember as MAN. If you haven't a clue as to whom you want to see when you arrive at a company's offices, always ask to see senior executives rather than middle or junior management – it's easier to start at the top and be passed down to the right level, if necessary, then to make your first contact at the bottom and work up.

OVERCOMING POSSIBLE OBSTACLES

Before actually achieving a face-to-face interview with a prospective buyer, possible obstacles could stand in your way in the form of the commissionaire/security, receptionist and the secretary or PA.

Keep a positive frame of mind throughout. Convince yourself that, as a genuine salesperson, getting in to see prospects isn't difficult and you're going to deal confidently, politely and firmly with anyone who stands in your way. After all, most of the difficulties are only in the mind of the salesperson who tends to imagine ones where none exists.

Getting past the commissionaire/secretary
- Don't walk up to the commissionaire hesitantly in a way that suggests you expect to be challenged and interrogated. Act naturally.

- Don't talk down to them.

- Keep to the point and ask directly for what you want.

- Act in an executive manner with an air of authority (this does not mean being arrogant and overbearing!).

Approaching the receptionist

These days receptionists can be either men or women. They are usually one of two types. The first is pleasant, helpful and good at dealing with people, but has limited powers of thought and observation. The second is an intelligent person, very observant and willing to help any visitor who creates the right impression with them. Your success at getting in without an appointment could depend on how quickly you suss out which type you find yourself facing at reception.

Things which irritate both types of receptionist and make them react unhelpfully to sales representatives are:

- A poor first impression.

- Being talked down to.

- A scruffy or poorly groomed appearance.

- Dirty hands and/or fingernails.

- Smoking while at the reception desk.

> **Most receptionists like salespeople to be positive and friendly without any kind of familiarity – not drongos!**

Dealing with objections

Whatever type of receptionist you find yourself facing, ask for exactly what you want without hesitation – just as though you fully expect to get it (which you will do, of course!) – and smile with your eyes. 'Good morning, could you tell Mr Jones that Colin Smith is here to see him, please?' And this is where you break off contact immediately by moving away from the reception desk and giving the impression by your manner that everything is arranged and cut and dried. Otherwise you give an opening to the receptionist to ask 'Do you have an appointment?' or some other question leading to the raising of an objection.

If you find yourself dealing with the more mature receptionist, it's wise to be ready with reasons for wanting to see the prospect, *but only use them if you're asked.* When faced with someone on reception whom you think might not convey messages correctly and is likely to spoil your chances of getting an interview, talk to the prospect direct on the house phone if possible.

Should you feel the receptionist is being unhelpful and obstructive, then:

- Ask to speak to the prospect's secretary or PA.

- Ask to speak to the prospect on the house phone.

- Phone the prospect or the prospect's secretary or PA from the nearest outside call box or on your mobile phone.

- Never let a receptionist win – don't give up. For your part, why not devote some thought as to why the receptionist is not being more helpful? Could the fault lie on your side?

ENLISTING THE HELP OF THE SECRETARY

It's the job of the secretary or PA to guard their boss from what appear to be 'time wasters' – unfortunately in the opinion of many secretaries salespeople arriving unannounced come into that category! But the secretary is the one who decides who is, and who isn't, a time waster. So, what influences them in making that decision?

It all comes down, as usual, to first impressions of you. In addition the secretary will need to be given

- a real and genuine reason – clearly and simply explained – for wanting to see the boss

- an assurance that only a short meeting is required and

- your diary visibly at the ready.

No doubt you will be able to think of other things that could be a positive influence in helping you towards that interview.

TO SUM UP

- Always treat a commissionaire, receptionist or secretary as courteously as possible.

- Don't do things that might annoy them, and double check your appearance.

- Never let any irritation you might be feeling show.

- Don't try to disguise the fact that you're a salesperson. You're a professional in your particular calling – be proud of it!

- Don't forget to smile, but don't overdo it.

- Don't let the receptionist win.

And remember on leaving to thank a receptionist, secretary, PA or assistant who has been helpful. This will be of great value in your future dealings with that company.

4

Pre-approach: the Preparation

Like the Scouts, be prepared and start the day right. By now it should be an established routine with you to:

- Check you briefcase. Have you all the material you're likely to need for each call?

- Understand what each specific call is for and what it entails.

- Decide on the maximum potential that can be gained from each call and what is the minimum acceptable to you.

- Decide what is the intermediate point of acceptable return between those two.

- Role play in your mind the likely scenario of the interview.

- Psyche yourself up and visualise yourself as being successful at each interview.

COMMENCING THE APPROACH

Let's take it that you've driven to your appointment and parked your car where you feel it's secure and accessible. If the interview with the prospect is likely to be a long one, don't park at a short-time meter. It'll cause you to worry and keep looking at your watch or, worse, rushing out at intervals to feed the meter. Check your planner, and think again of the purpose of your call, which is to get the order.

Walk briskly to your appointment with a spring in your step. Bear in mind that someone could be watching from the office window as you approach, so look relaxed and confident.

Being observant

Note such things as the building itself. Is it clean and modern? Does it give the impression that the company occupying it is progressive or perhaps a little behind the times? You can learn a lot from this general observation and it could give you a useful indication as to how you should proceed during the sales interview. The prospect handling buying for a company striving to be at the forefront with the latest technological advances needs a different approach from the buyer in an old-established family business to whom tradition and 'slow but sure' progress are all important.

Looking confident
When entering the building continue to walk briskly, remembering you are a professional salesperson who is thoroughly prepared for the interview ahead. You are confident of success because of the

---

- Be punctual.
- Be courteous.
- Ensure your appearance is neat.
- Don't drink until after your last call – one smells as much as several.
- Likewise, don't smoke.
- Smile confidently and look optimistic.
- Let the customer offer first to shake hands.
- Sit upright and alert.
- Avoid irritating mannerisms.
- Use the customer's first name only when invited to.
- Talk distinctly.
- Think first, talk last.
- Don't talk too much.
- Include the prospect and the prospect's interests in the conversation right from the start.
- Emphasise the 'you' angle.
- Don't try to be superior – the prospective customer knows the business better than you do.
- Don't discuss the prospect's competitors or criticise other purchases the prospect has made.
- Always tell the truth.
- Don't exaggerate or tell white lies.
- Demonstrate the highest respect and loyalty for your own company.
- By all means show you have a sense of humour, but don't try to be a comedian.
- And, finally, listen, listen and then listen – that way you'll learn much about the customer, the customer's business and the needs of the moment which ordinary questioning might not reveal.

Fig. 3. Making the approach: a checklist

preparation you have made and the faith you have in your product and service, which you know holds real benefit for the customer.

If you have an appointment, tell the receptionist who you are and whom you are there to see. Offer no other explanation or information. Be friendly, but maintain your authority. After you have introduced yourself move away from the reception desk and wait for the receptionist to phone your prospect to tell them you have arrived.

AND THE APPROACH ITSELF . . .

When you're in the presence of the prospect, remember that friendliness, attentiveness, helpfulness, tact and enthusiasm will help you win the day. A good approach, based on the checklist in Figure 3, will provide a sound base on which to build a successful sales interview.

TO SUM UP

Prepare yourself before the meeting. Approach the meeting looking confident and be observant of your surroundings. When you meet the prospect, remember to be friendly, attentive, helpful, tactful and enthusiastic.

5

The Approach

MAKING THE RIGHT IMPRESSION

> **You only have one opportunity to make a first impression –
> ensure it is positive.**

The objective of the approach is for you to empathise with the
prospect on meeting them and to create a favourable atmosphere for
the sales interview. It is therefore important that you

- make a favourable first impression on the prospect

- quickly check the pre-approach information you have is correct

- add to that information if necessary

- transform the prospect's existing favourable attention into positive interest in your product or service.

Once you've achieved all this, you can then confidently launch into
your sales presentation.

First impressions count

Many top-flight salespeople reckon the first few minutes are vital –
they can make or break a sale. If you've made a favourable first
impression, the prospect will respond by willingly listening to you.
When you meet a prospect for the first time, approach them with a
friendly smile and a firm handshake. Remember to speak clearly and
distinctly.

Getting the customer's name right

Make sure you know how to pronounce their second name correctly.
(We're familiar with Captain Mainwaring (Mannering), of *Dad's
Army* fame, and Mrs Bucket in *Keeping Up Appearances*, who calls
herself Bouquet, but names like Kerr and MacClean have alternative
pronunciations). An awkward or unusual one can be checked by a
quick call to their office beforehand. Switchboard operators are usually only too pleased to give help with names and titles. If you don't

know how to pronounce a second name, the person concerned will appreciate you saying so. They're used to other people having the same difficulty and 'Pardon my ignorance, but how do you pronounce your name?' can also prove a useful ice-breaker.

If you use a person's name it will make the sales meeting more friendly and less stiffly formal. Everyone likes to hear their own name, but don't overdo it. Never use the prospect's first name unless invited to do so. But when you introduce yourself, give both your first name and second name, so that the prospect can address you by whichever they prefer – aren't business cards wonderful!

Giving them your full attention

Early on in the discussion, take a sincere interest in the prospect's problems, hopes and wishes for the future. Show them you are there to help them benefit through the use of your product or service.

Keen attentiveness to what a person is saying is very flattering. If, in addition, you show respect for the prospect's position and maintain a friendly, sincere and helpful attitude, you'll be well on the way to a successful sale. Above all, be enthusiastic. If you act enthusiastically, the customer will mirror that enthusiasm.

THE CALL

Overcoming the barriers

If we take as an example the door-to-door salesperson, who could be selling anything from double glazing to dusters, brushes and floor polish, it is easy to understand the negative and defensive feelings of the householder opening the door to their knock. Could similar feelings be created in other less 'cold selling' situations, for example, where a salesperson calls on customers every week?

As a professional salesperson the only safe assumption you can make is that there *always* will be some form of barrier between you and each individual customer at the beginning of each call. And here we have to mention the exception to the rule, the salesperson who only aims at 'building up relationships' with customers and only ever 'chats' with them until they respond with an order. The order is not always given willingly – often it's to get rid of garrulous salespeople!

But how do truly professional salespeople, who seek respect and success instead of an easy life and popularity, successfully open their calls?

Opening the call

Here are the initial steps to opening the call and gaining the customer's attention and interest:

1. We have to get the customer's conscious agreement to talk business without any conscious or subconscious fears, reservations or feelings of being threatened and on the defensive.
2. We must ensure the customer sees the *benefit* to them and *wants to talk business.*

So, here you are, having greeted the customer with your full name and that of your company and using their second name and title. Your handshake is firm enough to indicate warmth and sincerity, but not bone crushing to make the customer wince. By the way, don't assume the customer will remember your name. Many salespeople are referred to among the office staff of companies they service only by the name of their product or service, such as 'Mr Mercury Vending' or 'Miss Butterfly Stationery'! Get the customer to remember your first name and second name and you'll know you've won attention and respect. Now from here take the following steps.

Making your reasons for being there clear

Should the reason for your visit not be clear at the introduction stage, always make a point of stating why you are there. One of the biggest builders of barriers results from a prospective customer knowing you're selling, but being unaware of what you want. Indeed there are some salespeople who totally misread this situation and try initially to conceal the reason for their call. This is taking the mystery and intrigue business a bit too far – nothing frightens people more than the 'unknown'.

Asking relevant questions and listening to the answers

Ask an open direct question on a subject related to the customer or the customer's business. For example, ask the customer how increased petrol costs have affected their business generally – don't ask specifically how sales of your own product have been affected. Questions about the customer's business will help remove any barriers between you by showing your genuine interest. *Listen* to the customer's answer.

Emphasising the benefits

Now follow up by offering the 'possibility' of something of *benefit to the customer*, e.g. 'I've got a couple of things to show you today, Mr Jones, that could well be of interest to you . . .'

Breaking down the barriers

Treat every customer as an individual, both in the way you open the call and the way you react to what they do. This is where empathy comes in. Look beyond the words you are hearing and try to judge what the customer is actually feeling. For instance the best way to handle a customer who begins with 'Don't talk to me about new products. I'm up to my eyes in new products and the salespeople trying to sell them to me ...' might be to respond just as aggressively (though respectfully) because you could be facing a person who enjoys a battle.

> **Always keep in mind that your prime objective during the first half a minute of a call is to break down any barriers and to sell yourself and the interview.**

Selling yourself as a professional

How do you do this? The tips in Figure 4 are based on what established customers and prospects had to say when asked what they thought constituted professionalism.

Respect for time: Be punctual and arrive on time for appointments. Ask open direct questions related to business, but don't then waste time by talking about irrelevancies. The customer is a busy person and so are you.

Credibility: Don't wildly exaggerate and make unsupported claims for your product or service. Its qualities will speak for themselves — just be sincere, honest and demonstrate the truth of the claims you can make for your product.

Competence: Show you know what you're doing and saying, and that you've done your homework and are adequately prepared for the interview. Nothing must be overlooked or forgotten. Important papers are of little use if left on your office desk or in the car, for instance.

Concern for the customer: Always think in terms of what's in it for the customer. Look at everything from the customer's angle. Show you are genuinely concerned in helping them and not simply after shifting some more of your products.

Fig. 4. What constitutes professionalism?

The first five minutes

Let's go over the first few minutes of the sales interview again. Here are some pointers to the opening:

- 'Good morning, Mr Jones. Tom Jenkins of YYY Company. Nice to meet you.'

- 'Thank you very much for letting me come and talk to you this morning. I'm sure that you are very busy and I appreciate your finding the time.'

- 'My reason for asking to see you is so that I can tell you about the services of YYY and to see if we can be of benefit to your company in the future.' (Soft and easy.)

- 'Before I tell you in detail about us, I wonder if I might raise a few points, so that I can understand more fully your likely needs?'

- 'Could I start off by asking . . . ?' (One or two questions.)

- 'I'll just make a note of that.' (It's always useful to have a record to which you can refer later – assume customer has no objections.)

Further questions:

- 'As I understand it . . .'
- 'The purpose of our meeting today is . . .'
- 'Before I tell you about us . . .'
- 'Could I ask . . . ?'

PROBING

The real skill in achieving a sale lies not just in guiding your prospect to making a decision in your favour. You must also lead them into believing they're not being sold to, but in fact have already make the right decision in coming to you.

Mastering the right questions and responses

Everyone uses questions naturally in everyday conversation. When selling, you must learn to ask the right questions naturally and to *listen to the answers*. Provided your questions are relevant, the response you'll get from the prospect will give you the opportunity to sell. That opportunity will fall into one of four categories:

1. An invitation from them for you to probe further in terms of need, authority and money (MAN), buying motives, timescales.

2. Reveal a chance for you to uncover an area of benefit or to seek agreement to a benefit.

3. Reveal an area of objection which you can further explore or overcome.

4. Provide an opportunity to close on your aims.

Remember: If you don't listen intelligently and perceptively, it will cost you a sale!

Preplanning your probing

Like everything else you do, you need to preplan to ensure you use the right probing questions. The more complete your knowledge in terms of MAN and timescales, the larger the number of the above opportunities you can create by your questioning. Your questions should also reveal or confirm an individual's buying motives, which can be taken into consideration before any visit. Bear in mind that buying motives can change between visits and can also be influenced or revealed by your persuasion. Understanding timescales will enable you to retain the initiative, so questions to reveal the timescale involved should be one of your first priorities.

As we've already agree, the first questions are always the most important, so direct them towards achieving that invitation to ascertain need, MAN, buying motives and timescales. The use of the right questions will

- create interest
- enable the prospect to see for themselves their true need
- reveal and confirm to you the prospect's buying motives.

Establishing what the buying motives are

These will often not be apparent to you – sometimes they're even unknown to your prospect. They are the underlying reasons, conscious or hidden, why a prospect reaches the decision in your favour. These reasons are sometimes irrational and, as already mentioned, can change between calls and are influenced by our selling. There'll be times, too, when you won't be able to offer relevant benefits that match your prospect's buying motives. Figure 5 lists some of the possible buying motives to watch out for.

Types of probe

There are two basic types of questions you can use when probing – both have been already touched on:

Price
- Savings
- Value for money
- Profits

Product
- Quality
- Appearance
- Versatility
- Ease of installation
- Durability
- Efficiency
- Safety
- Ease of maintenance

Service and backing
- Guarantees
- Advanced warning on any delays
- Design service
- Delivery (promised and maintained)
- Technical (call-out response)
- Information (from customer service department

Economy
- Labour (in terms of time)
- Increased efficiency
- Maintenance (level required)

Convenience
- Ease of ordering
- Availability of stock or replacements
- Ease of contact
- Product range

Safety
- Confidence (in product's performance, value for money, decision to buy)

Approval of others
- Regulatory bodies
- Staff
- Labour relations
- Higher management
- Lack of complaints
- Insurers

Prestige
- Purchasing the best
- Using the best British or European product

Competition
- Keeping up with competitors
- Getting ahead of competitors

Motivation of end-user
- Subcontractor's requirements

Fear (the most common motive)
- Freedom from any concerns or worries

Others include *standardisation, loyalty, urgency* or a *new requirements.*

Fig. 5. Buying motives.

1. *The closed probe* This is the direct question which invites a straight yes or no answer. Use it to get a reaction or seek agreement, for example, with 'I think this solves the problem, Mr Jones, don't you think . . . ?'

2. *The open probe* The open probe is used far more frequently to draw out information or an opinion from the prospect. It's the salesperson's most valuable tool. It starts with one of the following:

- Who?
- What?
- Where?
- Why?
- When?
- How?

Listening intelligently

Most people who are adept at talking, fail to take in what others are saying. To listen intelligently and perceptively you must develop the ability to penetrate the outer wrappings of the spoken word. People don't always say what they mean and you must be prepared for those prospects who find words inadequate when explaining their real needs.

Every conversation can be summed up like this:

- What each person has said.
- What they meant to say.
- What each person understood the other to say.

As regards listening, people do it in one of these ways:

- Bored inattention while waiting for the speaker to wind down.

- Listening only to classify what is being said, to place the speaker and what is said into a convenient mental pigeonhole.

- Judging what is being said so that it can be slotted into the listener's own preconceived ideas.

- Listening with eagerness (or ill-concealed impatience) waiting for the speaker to end – perhaps even breaking in and interrupting – so that the listener's own ideas or previous experiences can be imposed on the speaker.

If guilty of any of the above, you're listening only to what you'd like to hear, or expect to hear. As a professional and successful salesperson, you can't afford to listen like this.

ESTABLISHING NEEDS: GAINING INTEREST

Any sales presentation you make is considerably easier if the prospect has already accepted in their own mind a *need* for what you have to sell. This is the first mental step in your favour. If the customer feels – and is made aware by you – they've a problem or an opportunity of which to take advantage, and you have the solution, then they're bound to be *interested* in what you have to say. So we've then gained their *interest*, the next mental step.

Investigating the customer's needs

The stage between your opening statement, when hopefully you'll gain the customer's *attention*, and your presentation, which aims to gain *conviction*, *desire* and *action*, has the following objectives. To

1. achieve the mental step of interest and

2. discover what you need to know by ways of facts, figures, the attitude and mood of the customer (their buying motives) to enable you to make an effective presentation.

This stage could be termed needs investigation.

There will be times when, hopefully, the customer is already interested to a certain degree. Perhaps the sales interview is the result of the customer responding to your firm's advertisement, or receiving a personal recommendation, making them keen to hear what you have to offer. Often, however, you won't have gained the mental step of wholehearted *interest* you seek. It could be the customer is playing the field, testing the water or getting an update on the market. There could even be no money available in the budget for your product or service.

So you might find yourself having to work quite hard to turn round a passing interest – 'I'll listen to what you have to say, but I doubt if you can help us' – into serious interest. You'll probably still need, too, a great deal of information to know what to sell to the particular customer and how.

Developing your key skills

Here's where the key skills of your questioning and listening techniques will help you achieve the two objectives of the needs investigation stage. They'll get you information and create genuine interest on the part of the buyer. Let's look more closely at the objectives of the questions you will ask during the needs investigation. They are to:

- Make your presentation more effective by finding out relevant facts and figures, plus what's on the customer's mind at the moment.

- Get the customer relaxed and interested by showing a genuine interest in them and their business.

- Create an atmosphere more by way of a consultation than a sales meeting and show the customer you have shared objectives. You're not telling the customer, or selling to them. You're consulting them about their needs and offering to work with them to achieve results.

- Project your personality and credibility enough to make the customer feel able to consult you.

- Arouse certain dissatisfaction by making the customer look forward to your presentation and introducing some key benefits that make the customer realise there are some things they might not have realised they were missing out on.

- Identify the criteria for the sale, so you know what's best to try to sell the customer and how to accomplish this.

We again focus on the ability to ask the right questions as the key to successful selling. Without this you'll never find out what a prospective customer wants to buy or even if they want to buy at all. For the want of good questions, poor salespersons find their presentations going down like a lead balloon.

Consulting, not interrogating
There are two rules of human communication:

- People prefer talking to listening.
- People like to be consulted.

A salesperson who opens up with the right questions in a consultative manner will help put the customer at ease as well as gain valuable information. But here's a warning: people don't like to undergo interrogation-style questioning or to feel they're being manoeuvred solely for the benefit of the seller.

Do not rely on logic
Another reason why the consultative approach works well is the consistent failure of logic employed in trying to persuade people if they're not in the right mood. You've probably experienced it your-

self when trying to persuade partner or friend not to proceed with some course of action they're planning. You prove to them conclusively that what they intend to do can only end in tears. Try as you may, they show little interest in what you have to say and go ahead with their plans. All you said would happen comes about, but even then they're unrepentant.

Where you went wrong was in your approach – you assumed that logical argument would prevail. Your attempts at persuasion failed, however, and only made your partner or friend even more determined to follow the course of action.

Don't make out you could be wrong

What you really did was to succeed in telling them you were wrong and the more you proved this, the less chance you gave them of saving face and accepting your advice.

No one likes to be shown to be wrong – it's only human nature. Very few people will admit openly they are just simply and plainly wrong. Most of us will, however, accept there are alternative possibilities. If consulted as to what these possibilities might be, they then can be further guided towards your way of thinking.

Questioning is a two-way process

Selling with the help of questioning is a logical process to achieve logical and emotional objectives. Conducting the sale within a two-way methodical framework allows disparate views to be presented without meeting rigid resistance. You ask the customer first to define their problem in their own words and then to list the criteria to be taken into account for a satisfactory solution. This puts the customer at ease – it's their problem that's being discussed and their opinion that's being invited. The customer does most of the talking, but you come over as being on their side because you're showing interest, concern and willingness to assist.

An open and closed case

Here's where you learn and get necessary information by asking those **open questions**. you know, the ones preceded by

- 'What . . . ?'
- 'Why . . . ?'
- 'When . . . ?'
- 'Where . . . ?'
- 'How . . . ?'
- 'Who . . . ?'

which cannot be answered by a plain 'yes' or 'no'. An example is 'How do you think this will be of benefit to you?' The customer can't help but tell you what they think – and why.

Closed questions, you will remember, begin with words like

- 'Do ...?'
- 'Can ...?'
- 'Have ...?'
- 'Will ...?'

You can use them to gain a commitment from the customer, such as 'Do you think this quality of product will be more economical in the future for you?'

Both open and closed questions can be phrased in such a way to be **direct** or **indirect**. Direct questions can be used when you're quite happy for the customer to know the purpose of your question, such as:

- 'What do you think of the salesperson who calls on you?'

Indirect questions are a more subtle and roundabout way of getting information, particularly when you think the customer's personal attitude could colour the answer, for example:

- 'Are there any ways by which we can improve our service to you?'

Using prompt questions
Success with the consultative style of selling depends on you showing interest and concern for the customer. The best way of achieving this is by openly showing how interested you are in what *the customer* is saying. A natural way of doing this is by occasional comments such as 'Really?' or 'Good Lord!' But a more controlled way of achieving the same result is with *reflective questioning*, by which you 'mirror' what the other person is saying.

Questioning reflectively
This again is a technique which, because it slips naturally and smoothly into the conversation, is rarely recognised as a sales technique. And it's essential that any selling technique isn't obvious as such to a customer, because it immediately loses its value and the credibility of the sales person goes out of the window. All you do with reflective questioning is to repeat the last phrase of a key phrase the customer has said with a query in your voice. For example: '... and we are planning a new production line in the New Year.' 'A new production line?'

By doing this you demonstrate interest and indicate you are

listening intently. If the customer has mentioned two or three points, this technique also enables you to choose the one you wish to pursue in order to control the direction of the interview along the route most beneficial to you, the seller. As a professional salesperson you'll be able to get all the information you want in regard to facts, figures and the attitude and mood of the prospect. In this way you'll be able to control the customer's input into the discussion without the customer even knowing.

Listening reflectively

This is where you show you're not only interested in what the customer has been saying, but have been listening intelligently to what they have to say. You summarise something the customer has said with an impressed tone in your voice:

- 'So your company is increasing production in the New Year?' Then follow up immediately with another question:

- 'Does this mean you'll be expanding in other fields?'

Perhaps of most importance in questioning technique is not so much the actual words used, but the style and manner you adopt. After all, questions can be threatening or complimentary, depending on the way you put them over.

Obtaining the customer's interest and trust

Skilful questioning can serve a double purpose – not only feeding you with vital information but also gaining the customer's interest and trust. First *know* your customer. This means finding out all you can about them and their business. Carefully framed questions can enable you to get information necessary for you to prepare your case. But while this is important, always bear in mind that at the same time you should be seeking by your questions to create interest and relax the customer:

- *Judge* the mood of the customer.

- Express *concern* and *empathy*, and ask the customer's *opinions* by way of showing genuine respect.

- Let your approach be *consultative*, never overbearing, threatening or coercing.

- *Agree* with the customer – without creeping or crawling.

- Above all, *listen* carefully to what the customer has to say.

When you're satisfied you've uncovered or revealed to the customer all their needs and have gained their interest, you can proceed with your presentation. But as a professional you'll keep up the questioning throughout the complete sales interview. You'll want continuous feedback so that where necessary you can be flexible and go with the mood of the moment to achieve that all-important commitment from the customer – first to your ideas and finally, of course, when you're closing and asking for the order.

Questions during a sales presentation

Aim to make the presentation a dialogue with an exchange of information, not a monologue on your part. Ask one question at a time and, early on, make the questions relevant, to make it quite clear in the customer's mind as to the reason you are there. The customer must see these questions as reasonable and not too probing, personal or confidential, so use indirect questions.

The first stage in the presentation is the introduction, so be ready with:

- All necessary information known and effective open questions prepared.
- A good opening statement that will help the customer relax, accept you and give you their attention.

- An open indirect question to show the customer you are interested in them.

Now comes the investigation into the customer's needs. Achieve this by:

- Following up with a question any statement you make, especially if it's regarding a benefit to the customer.

- Answering any question put to you briefly, but enough to satisfy the customer, then in turn asking a related question (not too probing, however).

- Making good use of prepared open questions which progressively become more direct, to get the customer interested and talking freely and openly.

- Using closed questions to clarify points and elicit commitment.

Again, employ good listening techniques by:

- Actively listening and showing keen interest in the customer's contribution to the discussion.

- Making notes to demonstrate your interest.

- Using reflective questions to keep a measure of control if the customer is contented to talk freely. This is fine. It means they're interested, but don't risk things by being flexible and stolidly keeping to your original plans.

Points to remember during the main part of the presentation are:

- To start asking direct questions to identify the customer's needs to them, making them feel dissatisfied enough to do something about it.

- Easy questioning for feedback as you make your presentation.

- Closed, but indirect questions to gain the customer's commitment to the idea of what you are suggesting.

- Closed, direct questions to get the order.

TO SUM UP

The approach.
We can best remember all the qualities of a good approach with the mnemonic **FATHE**:
F   Friendliness
A   Attentiveness
T   Tact
H   Helfulness
E   Enthusiasm.

The golden rules for opening the call
- First sell the interview – not the product or service.
- Sell yourself – as a professional salesperson.
- Demonstrate your concern for the customer and an interest in them and their business.
- Show you are aware that time is money.
- Be positive.

Selling is not telling
To achieve a successful selling interview, you as the seller must spend more time listening than talking. You'll find these guidelines on perceptive listening helpful. Listen:

- *With an open mind, acceptance and positive interest in what the other person is saying.* Keep that interest alive throughout and reserve any judgement until you have all the facts.

- *With expectancy*, waiting for the full picture to be revealed as seen through the eyes of your prospect.

- *With involvement and understanding of the prospect's feelings*, not just their words which might not convey what your prospect means.

Aiming for two-way communication

The 'gift of the gab' is not the only thing that makes a good salesperson. Of course, a professional must be able to talk fluently and intelligently but, as we've stressed before in this book, being a good listener is just as important. Yes, it can be disconcerting when the customer breaks in with a comment or question just as you're getting into your stride. But with what you've now learned about questioning techniques you will be able to turn interruptions like these to your advantage.

All too often someone considered a good salesperson will press on without giving the customer a chance to get a word in edgeways. However, the successful salesperson who walks away with a definite commitment from the customer is the one who gets *two-way communication* going. Training yourself to listen, but still control the interview by skilful questioning, will pay good dividends.

6

Conditions for Ordering

You've worked hard on your initial research, you've made all the right moves to gain an interview and now you're face to face for the first time with the prospective buyer. In general terms you have a shrewd idea what their requirements are, but you are now going to go more deeply into these. Most buyers have in mind certain conditions by which they judge the suitability or otherwise of a product or service. Your task now is gently to tease out of the prospect what those conditions are and, in order to secure an order now or in the future, persuade them your product or service meets all these requirements.

What appears to be a tentative exploratory meeting on your part in the early stages should finish up with you being requested to quote or at least favoured as a supplier when next the buyer needs to place an order. The general principles are the same whether you're selling office furniture or soap powder. But for the moment let's suppose your company supplies computing systems used for financial and stock control, where performance, delivery and installation are factors that come into play.

Once asked to list their conditions for ordering, you'll find most buyers are only too pleased to tell you what they expect of a product or service as far as price, performance and delivery are concerned. These are the three things that are top of most lists. Aftersales backup services and technical support are also important considerations.

First, always ask the buyer if they mind you getting their list of conditions for ordering down on paper. If it turns out to be a long and complicated list, it's essential you have a note of their conditions. It will also come in useful later on when, for the buyer's benefit, you show them what your company can do compared with existing suppliers.

ESTABLISHING THE TOP CONDITIONS OF THE ORDER

Price and value for money
Price will most likely be the buyer's first consideration. Coupled with this is value for money. So start off by asking the buyer whether they

tend to look for the lowest price or are more concerned with ensuring they get the best all-round value for their money. Add that you're thinking here in terms of lower maintenance and running costs. You can confidently bet they'll plump for value for money – few buyers will admit they look for the lowest price!

Performance – can it do the job?

The next consideration will be performance, particularly in the case of computing systems. Do hardware and specially adapted software programs do the job intended? Here you will want to find out from the buyer if:

- they tend to keep rigidly to their own specification or ideas or

- they look to the supplier to come up with suggestions for better ways of doing the job or less expensive ways of getting the same – or perhaps better – results.

The buyer might secretly think they always know best, but when it comes to the crunch they'll more than likely accept they've got to leave some technical details to others. So you'll probably find the buyer will go for the second of the options listed above.

Delivery

When questioning the buyer about conditions they've established in respect of delivery, you'll be able to find out to what degree the buyer expects a supplier to fit in with their own office or manufacturing site schedule. Particularly in the case of computing systems, where equipment isn't the sort you can readily supply 'from stock' but is tailored for each customer, planning and layout are involved. Both sides will want to avoid as much disruption as possible.

AMPLIFYING YOUR NOTES

All the time you've been sounding out the buyer, you should have been adding more details to the notes you've been busily making as the interview has progressed. 'Flesh out' your notes something like this:

- *Price* – not worried too much about how much it costs, provided it gives the best value for money.

- *Performance* – system must do the job intended, but customer would welcome suggestions for simpler, less costly ways of achieving the same results or even better ones.

• *Delivery* – expects delivery to fit in with own staff arrangements.

Having covered the essentials, you can now move on to complete the remainder of your list. With a little gentle prompting and help from you, the buyer will reveal other criteria for ordering which will enable you to build up the list and increase your chances of getting new business.

Perhaps you could start by asking the buyer to agree they look for equipment that will perform to specification and performance for a number of years without any problems. Once you've received an assenting nod from the buyer, you can add *reliability* and *longest trouble-free operation* to your list of criteria. With some more gentle prompting, the buyer will similarly respond with regard to *lowest running and maintenance costs*, which you can then add to the list.

You then enquire whether the buyer's own computer systems manager and technical staff will be planning the layout of the network and handling the actual installation themselves – plus testing and getting the system up and running? No such qualified staff or 'tame' in-house team of experts available? Good! The buyer will be looking for a supplier who can handle these operations and take them off their hands. Your company's ability to take charge of all aspects of the installation could aid you justifying a higher price for the computer system. Add to your list *design, layout and installation – must all be done by supplier capable of providing complete package.*

Has the buyer considered the next important aspect – space? Is the computing system to take up as little room as possible in the buyer's office or factory storeroom? The buyer wants to preserve as much space as possible, so write down *absolute minimum space*. Then there's the question of staff relations. Has the buyer thought about the impact of the Health and Safety at Work Act? Will the trade unions or staff associations consider adequate precautions have been taken with the working environment to ensure the health and safety of the operators at the computer terminals? Sitting position, viewing height of the computer screen, anti-glare devices – yes, the buyer believes in *ensuring and improving working conditions for staff*. Another item for your criteria list.

From the buyer, too, you'll elicit confirmation they won't take on any new product or service unless the supplier can guarantee full technical support and backup services. *Reliable aftersales and technical advice services important* will go on the list. Also now's the time to sound the buyer out and confirm they would grant an order only to a well established company with a reputation for reliability and fair dealing (surprisingly very much like the one you represent!) – note down *stability, reliability and reputation.*

Your company and its salespeople pride themselves in making contact – and in keeping in contact with customers. You stress that as a supplier your company understands individual customer's requirements and acts on them promptly. Everyone in the office and out in the sales field is trained to be a good communicator. Perhaps the buyer hadn't thought up to this point how important *communication* is, but can't help but agree it should be on the list of criteria.

Raising the question of *ethics* gives you the opportunity to blow your company's trumpet. Put it to the buyer the supplier has the choice of concentrating on what they're selling or on the customer. Is the salesperson really interested in providing the best computing system to solve a customer's problems and achieve their objectives, or are they just interested in selling as many systems as possible? Here's where you, hand on heart, say you have always believed the customer is the most important person in your company's business – an integral part of the company philosophy. The buyer is bound to agree that this philosophy should be taken into consideration.

THE COMPLETE LIST

If all has gone smoothly, you should have a list of the criteria (see Figure 6) which influence this particular buyer when they are making a decision involving ordering. Always leave a copy of these criteria with the customer when you leave. Now you know what the customer looks for, there are two courses open to you:

- Plunge in and prove to them you can meet all these requirements and, once you've done this, get them to agree to include your company among suppliers of computing systems asked to quote for future work.

- Ask the customer which suppliers they use and suggest a comparison between these and your own company against each of the criteria on the list by drawing vertical columns – one for each supplier – on your pad, together with a separate column for your company, like the example given in Figure 7. (Remember discuss your company's merits first, before that of your rivals – in case time runs out.)

CLOSING THE CONVERSATION

After you've proved to the customer your company is a good proposition as a supplier of their future requirements, end the conversation

- *Price* — is concerned more with getting best value for money than price itself.
- *Performance* — system must do the job intended for it, but would welcome simpler or less expensive layout and programming to achieving the same or better results.
- *Delivery* — has to fit in with buyer's schedules involving minimum disruption to office and other staff.
- *Reliability* — longest trouble-free service that's possible, plus low costs and ease of maintenance.
- *Design, layout and installation* — supplier must be able to handle everything from initial planning to setting up fully operational system.
- *Space* — the absolute minimum.
- *Staff* — everything must be taken into account to ensure good working environment meeting health and safety requirements.
- *Stability of supplier* — supplier must have sound business reputation and good aftersales servicing arrangements.
- *Communications* — essential at all times between customer and supplier before, during and after installation of system.
- *Ethics* — respects a supplier who puts customer, not product, first.

Fig. 6. The complete list of conditions.

My company	CRITERIA	Supplier A	Supplier B
Always best value	PRICE	Reasonable	Hidden extras
Second to none	PERFORMANCE	Criticised on occasions	Lived up to promise

Always discuss your company's merits before that of your rivals — in case time runs out.

Fig. 7. Making comparisons.

by asking the customer when they expect to install the next computing system and when they would like you to call round. Don't miss the chance either of underlining your wish to remain in contact by asking if there is anything you can do in the mean time or show the customer now. Always make sure, too, there isn't anyone else you should be talking to.

If the customer shows they are more than happy to consider you as a good supplier, it would be worthwhile suggesting a visit to the office or factory to look at the actual requirements. It will impress the prospective client you're really on the ball and also feed you vital information regarding what other suppliers have suggested.

Now it's a question of waiting and seeing what happens. Preparing a list of the conditions a customer lays down when ordering doesn't always work, and sometimes only partially. But don't despair and go into a decline if it doesn't. You will have achieved something, even if it's only to use the parts you succeed in getting down. Don't give up. As that trite but encouraging old saying tells you: 'If at first you don't succeed, try, try and try again.' Nothing is a foregone conclusion in selling, and it is this that's the fascinating thing about the challenging but enjoyable calling we follow as salespeople.

TO SUM UP

Establish the customer's top priorities for an order – those will usually include price, performance and delivery. Write down other conditions the prospect specifies and amplify these as the meeting progresses. If you compare your company's merits with those of rivals, discuss your company's merits first in case you run out of time. End the conversation with an agreement to talk in the near future.

---

8 RULES FOR SALESPEOPLE

1. *You sell at a price determined by me.*
2. *You provide free point of sale material.*
3. *You refund all goods that fail to sell.*
4. *You send goods even if you are out of stock.*
5. *You provide unlimited return authorisation slips.*
6. *You provide free sales training for our staff.*
7. *You pay delivery charges to our store.*
8. *You pay for advertising your products in our catalogue.*

Signed: the buyer

---

maybe we should find a way to wrap up delivery costs of equip within price

7

Selling Benefits

DEFINING THE BENEFITS

The dictionary defines *benefit*, among other things, as an advantage. In the sales sense there's no advantage to be gained until a product or service offering benefits is actually used. Many features of a product or service are of advantage, and the salesperson should always translate these into terms of benefits to the customer.

The way to go about this is to list all:

- the integral features of your firm's product or service
- the technical features
- the features of the aftersales service

and then, for each of the above, list:

- the benefits to be derived from each feature and build them into each and every sales presentation you make.

KEEPING THE COMMUNICATION GOING

Let's go over the basic points we've already learned regarding presentations, remembering to talk clearly and unhurriedly, using strong positive language:

- Selling is a two-way communication process, so *listen*.

- Show warmth, sincerity, but above all *enthusiasm*.

- Personalise your approach so that you talk in terms of the customer and their problems by using *you*.

- Talk in simple language, cut out technical terms and *avoid jargon*.

- Find out the customer's real wants and needs.

- Be accurate, shun exaggeration, produce proof and show your honesty.

- Use literature, models and samples to help you *demonstrate*.

- Let the customer feel, smell, touch, see for themselves the *practical aspects*.

Always talk in terms of what the product or service will do for your listener, the customer. Buyers won't necessarily be impressed by what you or I think. They'll be more impressed if you tell them what the product will do for them – its benefits. For example: 'You will find that . . .' or 'You will see that . . .' Don't talk down to customers or lecture them. At the same time, don't take it for granted they know what you're talking about and are following the point you're trying to make. If there's the slightest doubt, qualify your comment with: '. . . which, as you most likely know, means that . . .' or '. . . which you've probably come across before . . .'

Watch for any signs of agreement or doubt. Look at the customer's eyes, gauge their mood, observe the way they're sitting. Obtain their agreement as you go along so that you've got the green light to continue with your presentation.

WHAT THE CUSTOMER MAY BE INTERESTED IN

There are likely to be over-riding requirements particular to certain customers, but each customer is likely to be interested in other aspects dependent on their own needs, attitudes and interests. Although it's not possible to classify each of these, we can look at them generally, as follows:

EFFICENCY – effectiveness, performance.
NOVELTY – unique, new, outstanding unusual characteristics.
SAFETY – buying from a reputable company, also safety of equipment.
CONVENIENCE – ease of ordering, communication and other facilities.
APPEARANCE – design, general appeal.
DURABILITY – lasting, reliable, sturdy.
ECONOMY – good investment, savings, profit.

These initial letters give us another handy mnemonic to aid our memory: **ENSCADE**.

Too many salespeople praise the features of the product, but not the benefits in terms of what's in it for the customer. So:

- List all particular features of the product or service.
- Describe all the general features of the backup services available.
- Translate these into benefits under each heading of **ENSCADE**, expressing them in terms of what's in it for the customer.

- Commit these benefits to memory.
- Identify which aspects of **ENSCADE** will be of prime interest to the customer.
- Express all the benefits you have remembered under the appropriate headings.

EXAMPLES OF BENEFITS

One feature of a product or service can be expressed as several benefits. As our first example, let's say there's a new type of machine on the market for production-line work – it doesn't matter what its function is, any machine will do – and you're setting out to show a prospective customer the benefits to be derived from buying such a machine. Let's further imagine that the driving shaft of the machine has been made thicker than previous models, a feature you're going to translate into benefits to the buyer.

Major benefits will be as follows:

- *Safety* – no fears of metal fatigue or the shaft cracking up due to overload, because it has been designed and tested to take increased loading stress.

- *Durability* – the shaft's robust design means longer life.

- *Economy* – a greater running life resulting from the ruggedness of the shaft means in turn greater productivity from the customer's investment.

- *Novelty* – it's the only machine of its kind on the market which offers the advantage of a more robust, durable shaft.

For our second example we'll take the way a product is packaged for the consumer selling market. The product can be anything from a kitchen utensil to a toy, but the important feature is that it's packaged in a stout box with a transparent firm plastic lid. Now to translate this feature into benefits:

- *Convenience* – the uniform design of the package makes storage and handling easier, so that when stacked it's less likely to topple over.

- *Safety* – the stout packaging guards against the product being crushed while being stored or handled.

- *Appearance* – the package is designed to attract the consumer, so it acts as a promotional aid.

- *Durability* – the carefully designed package keeps the product in good condition, and the box itself doesn't get bent or creased.

- *Economy* – the package is designed so that storage space is kept to a minimum. Furthermore, because of its appeal to the consumer, the package helps to increase turnover.

By doing this exercise for every feature of the product you are selling, you will arrive at a list of benefits expressed in terms of what's in it for the customer.

SELLING THE BENEFITS

Don't be tempted to put the cart before the horse, however. There's a great temptation to rush into selling the benefits before you've given the customer the complete picture regarding your product or service. Introducing possible benefits too early on in your presentation could well lead to objections rather than decisions.

DEVELOPMENT IN FOUR STAGES

Employing the four-stage development outlined below will ensure you have the best possible chance of success in any selling situation. While it cannot perform the impossible and create benefits where none exists, progressing through these stages will lead to more decisions in your favour.

- *First*, it's important to understand the current situation before introducing features or apparent benefits.

- *Secondly*, take into account the buying motives of the customer. Remember, these can vary and influence decisions.

- *Thirdly*, remember that selling features alone is pointless and sounds expensive unless backed up by the benefits.

- *Fourthly*, benefits only exist where they are relevant to the particular customer to whom you are selling.

SOURCES OF BENEFITS

All these aspects of products, services, company and staff can produce benefits to customers:

- *Products* – delivery, workmanship, mobility, design, operation, stocks, components, credit, packaging, appearance.

- *Services* – speed, presales advice, installation, availability, maintenance, training, guarantees, credit, merchandising, advertising, aftersales service.

- *Company* – length of time established, philosophy, reputation, labour relations, policies, location, size, financial standing.

- *Staff* – knowledge, availability, skill, training, character, specialists.

TO SUM UP

Translate your product's benefits into benefits for the customer. Listen to what the customer wants and make sure you stress how your product's benefits can meet these requirements. Remember, a benefit only exists where it is relevant to a particular customer.

8

Objections, the Competition and Absent Authorities

HANDLING OBJECTIONS

We're now ready to look in more detail at how objections raised by prospective customers can be recognised and dealt with successfully. What attitude should you adopt towards objections? As professional salespeople we learn from any setback or problem and look upon it as an opportunity for us to exercise our ingenuity. So looking at objections is a positive manner we find that we can:

- Accept them as normal, inevitable interruptions during the sales interview.

- Look upon them as an indication of the propsect's interest.

- Welcome them as a means of telling us the attitude and needs of the customer, and how well they're understanding the presentation.

Classifying objections

We can classify objections into three main categories (see Figure 8):

- *Valid objections* are those that reveal customer's real worries regarding such things as fear of making the wrong choice, justifying the need or the cost involved, and often a search for reassurance on the part of the prospect.

- *Invalid objections* can be trifling excuses disguising attempts to play for time, or reluctance to surrender without putting up some resistance, but they can result from blind prejudice.

- *Hidden objections* have to be brought to the surface by careful questioning.

False objections

There are also what we'll term 'false' objections. These are attempts to get rid of you or fend you off. They can arise at any time in a presentation if the customer feels you're trying to manoeuvre them against their will or you're being too aggressive with your sales pitch.

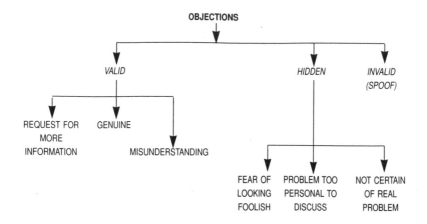

Fig. 8. Classifying objections.

But this type of objection comes usually . . .

- At the beginning . . . Most of us have made excuses to door-to-door sellers – or even told white lies – to get rid of them. Occasionally there will be a customer who also responds in this way if they think you're selling hard too soon, or they're busy and just don't feel like being sold to.

- Or at the close . . . If a customer hasn't reached that point in the sales interview where they want to make a firm commitment, they will probably respond to your close with all kinds of weak excuses.

Recognising false objections
Often you'll find it difficult to differentiate between real and false objections, but here are two sure ways to find out.

Rely on your own judgement
If you're listening intelligently to the customer and observing their body language, more often than not you'll realise when they're fending you off.

Test the water
In effect you base the sale on the objection, like in a trial close where you would say, 'If I can show you the problem doesn't exist, would you be interested?' For instance, in reply to the customer's objection that your product or service is too expensive, your reply would be: 'If I could show you a deal that makes the price less than what you're using now, would you be interested?' The customer's response should

tell you whether they really mean what they say. A reply like, 'that's all very well, but I'm not interested in taking on any new lines', would clearly indicate the customer has no intention of buying at the moment and is making excuses.

If the customer says, 'If you can bring the price down, I'd certainly give it consideration', then you can go on to deal with their objection because you know it's a genuine one.

It's important to face up to the fact that a false objection is a symptom of *lack of interest* and that could be down to you and no fault of the customer's. One way or another, you've got to back pedal to try to get the customer off the defensive, which could be easier said than done.

If the customer doesn't really believe in the false objection they've raised, you're wasting your time – and theirs – if you enter into a discussion on the subject. So ignore it and concentrate on winning back the customer to your way of thinking. One way of doing this is simply to agree with the customer by replying with an innocuous statement or question. For example, if the false objection is to the effect that their own customers prefer a higher-quality product, you would reply something like this: 'Yes, Mr Jones, customers can be pretty choosy. How would you say your sales of top-quality products compare with those of less expensive ones?'

Isolating the valid objection

Many salespeople know the answers to most objections they're likely to meet. Normally, however, customers raise a lot of objections that don't represent the real reason for them refusing the buy. As we've seen, false objections that are really put-offs need never be answered.

When handling valid or genuine objections, you'll find the following phrases of value:

- '. . . apart from . . .'
- 'Let's assume that . . .'
- 'Let's suppose that . . .'
- '. . . and if that were not the case . . .'

So if we take the example above, where the customer objected on the grounds of the product being expensive, you might have well answered: 'What do you feel about the product *apart from the cost*, Mr Jones?'

To which the customer might well reply, 'Well, we're satisfied with our present supplier'.

'*Let's assume that* I could prove our product offers you the advantages of better quality and service, would you then be happy to order from us, Mr Jones?' And hopefully the customer will give you a change to prove it and agree to give you an order. The objection on the grounds of price was, of course, a false one, and has been handled positively to good effect by enabling you to show your product in a better light than that of its competitor.

Overcoming objections

Think of any objections you encounter as being very like obstacles in the path of a traveller. If you're to teach your ultimate goal, you have to learn to handle the objections barring your way to a successful sale. Like a traveller, too, you should be prepared and take advantage of the experience gained by other salespeople before you and contained in the pages of this book.

Both valid and invalid objections should be tackled in exactly the same way. Treat both seriously, even though you might feel the objections are unfounded – they could be very real to the customer making them. Don't rule out the possibility the customer could be putting you in the hot seat to soften you up, for instance, a price cut.

Objections commonly encountered are

- price
- loyalty to an existing supplier
- reluctance to make an instance decision
- bad experience in past dealings with your company
- dislike of your company group
- dislike of you
- proposition is considered not good enough.

Some golden rules to be observed in handling objections are

- listen
- empathise
- don't argue
- be sure you understand what the objection is about; if not, ask
- welcome valid objections as indications of customer interest
- ignore false objections and aim to regain customer's attention and interest.

Advancing your case

Professional salespeople look upon objections not with apprehension but as a help and means of advancing their case. So to make the most of the opportunities presented by objections you must possess

- a positive attitude
- knowledge of the answers
- objection-handling skill.

An objection in the sales sense has been defined as 'any question, statement, expression, action or state of mind that interrupts the progress of a sale'. And it's important to bear in mind that an objection is not necessarily in the form of words. Your customer or prospect can express objection by

- silence
- lack of agreement
- a look of indifference
- bored expression
- tone of voice
- 'yes' said grudgingly.

Planning your presentation and preparing answers to possible objections, of course, will mean that rather than just having to concentrate on what to say, you'll be able to watch for the above warning signs.

Your attitude is vitally important. You could look upon the prospective customer as either deliberately being difficult or obstructive in order to defeat you, but this would be entirely negative on your part. Accent the positive and eliminate the negative by regarding the prospect who objects as assisting you to arrive at a mutually satisfactory conclusion.

When a customer objects, it will be for a reason. Either they're seeking further information or seeking justification to buy. Most objections are helpful and necessary for you to get the order. They're usually an indication of the customer's interest, albeit that it's expressed in negative terms.

They are helpful because they:

- *Indicate whether the prospective customer is hot or cold in their response.* They show what the existing situation is, the prospect's state of mind in relation to you, your proposition and the environment.

- *Point to the customer's area of interest.* Of prime importance, this enables you to isolate and focus on the reason or reasons why the customer is going to buy.

- *Reveal the presence of any competition.* It's important to know this, because it's very probable your competitors will have angled their sales pitch to highlight their advantages over what they claim are your disadvantages.

• *Indicate buying signals.* You cannot fail to see and hear these if you're interacting effectively and communicating well with the customer. Once you've recognised them, if you handle them correctly, they'll afford you opportunities to close.

Some objections do nothing towards the successful outcome of a sale. They're ones you yourself will have created.

Poor presentation
Poor product presentation or handling can raise a genuine objection in the mind of the customer. If you say your product is easy to use, make sure you show it in demonstration!

Too technical an explanation
It's easy to forget you're a specialist when it comes to your own product and its application. You may well be among people who are also specialist in their own particular fields, but don't assume they have the same technical understanding of your product and its application. So aim for simplicity and never attempt to get one over other people with your technical knowledge.

Not listening properly
Listen carefully and give the right answers to questions from the customer. Wrong or off-the-mark answers not only prolong sales interview – they can also give rise to argument and objections.

Misrepresentation
As a professional salesperson you would never be guilty of this deliberately, but guard against it happening inadvertently as the result of errors of omission, poor communication or getting too carried away with enthusiasm.

Wrong application or benefits
Failure to identify a customer's real needs and sometimes lack of pre-call planning can find you trying to sell to them on the basis of the wrong application and the wrong benefits. The customer will most certainly reject them and you'll lose credibility in their eyes.

Emphasis on negative aspects
Make sure you speak of your product in positive terms. Don't, for instance, tell the customer your company revamped a machine

because of design faults. Instead, talk in terms of a new design for greater ease of operation and trouble-free service.

The relaxed approach

Don't be laid back, but certainly practise being relaxed when facing objections. You'll then be in the right frame of mind to handle them. Granted it's difficult to relax when you feel you're under fire, but settle yourself back in the chair and let this action and your demeanour give the customer the message: 'Go ahead and talk. I welcome anything you have to say. Tell me how you see it. What is your point of view?'

First let the customer state their objection fully. And make certain you listen, not just to the words, but to the nuances in the voice – seeking to interpret the undertones and overtones. It's a bit like tuning in a radio. Don't let your concentration flag and at the same time beware of being overanxious to crush the prospect's objection with your dazzling answer.

By allowing the customer to state their objection fully, you find out what the objection is and understand why they feel as they do. There's a therapeutic aspect, too. In stating their objection, the customer is releasing tension – 'getting it off their chest' – with the effect of lessening the objection in their own mind. But don't attempt to challenge the customer's objection at this point, because they will harden their opinion.

It pays to ask questions of the customer even if you're sure you know what the objection's about. Make them open questions, beginning with

- 'What'
- 'Why'
- 'When'
- 'Where'
- 'Who'
- 'How'.

As you're aware, these questions will give you information about how the customer really feels, enable you to find out the basis of the objection and learn the true objection, which is sometimes hidden, while providing other useful facts to add to your profile of the customer and their company.

This is what we mean by 'handling' an objection. It's falling into step with your customer and creating a friendly, co-operative atmosphere before you try to provide an answer. It's not always wise, however compelled you may feel, to try to answer all objections at once.

Handling and answering objections

There's a difference between 'handling' objections and 'answering' them. When objections arise you must take into consideration there exists, as with any communication situation between people, both an emotional and factual content. This emotional content will be present in both buyer and salesperson. When putting forward their objection, the buyer will be expressing a belief they firmly hold. True, partly true or untrue, it will probably make you react defensively. You'll have to 'handle' this situation before attempting to 'answer' the objection.

Often it's better to defer answering the objection until later on if:

• It breaks the set, logical sequence of your presentation when you're putting over the points you wish to make in the best possible order.

• By doing so you're losing the initiative.

• You haven't the answer and need time to think about it or refer back to your office.

If you do decide to defer answering, do it in a polite and acceptable manner by telling the prospective buyer you understand their point and it's a good one which you will answer later on in the presentation. Make sure you do answer it as promised, otherwise the prospect will think it's one you can't answer and will lose confidence in you.

There are occasions when you should answer an objection immediately. These are when:

• It is pertinent to the subject under discussion.
• It discloses an area of interest or a need.
• The buyer insists on an answer.
• Answering presents you with an opportunity to close.

Pre-handling

This again raises the value of planning to anticipate likely objections and neutralise them before they arise, which is termed pre-handling. The buyer, having shown commitment to a point of view by objecting, will see the need to defend it. Few people like to be proved wrong and the buyer can be antagonised if you demolish their argument. The art of pre-handling is to include in your sales story answers to possible objections before the prospect has a chance to voice them. The fewer the objections, the more speedy the sale.

But when you do have to give an answer, make sure it is the right one. No amount of glib words or attempts to blind your listener with science will save you. Here again, we can see the importance of pre-call and presentation planning.

Coming to a close

When you answer an objection, agree before you disagree. Stay cool and calm and guard against any inner annoyance or irritation you might be feeling betraying itself in your voice or face. You are at the proof stage, where you need to convince and satisfy the prospect that the promised benefits will indeed be realised. Very often, though, words are not enough, so support your words with

* visual aids
* supplementary literature
* samples, where applicable
* demonstration.

Third-party references supported by written testimonials, if available, alternative benefits, comparisons . . . use everything you can to back up your sales story.

  With all this, the prospect might be forgiven for missing one or two salient points, so it's often very useful to summarise at this stage for their benefit and yours. The buyer is going to make a decision on the basis the benefits will outweigh the price. The summary should serve the purpose of ensuring the buyer remembers all the benefits when it comes to 'make up mind' time.

OVERCOMING COMMON OBJECTIONS

Following on from the previous section we can list the most common objections as follows:

* price
* loyalty to an existing supplier
* bad past experience with your company
* dislike of your company
* dislike of you
* your proposition isn't good enough.

There are simple rules for answering objections, most of which you'll find you're using at present – and probably have been for some time. Continue with them, but from now on make yourself consciously aware of them, and analyse and think about them. Once again, a helpful mnemonic – **READY** – comes to our aid:

REVERSE
EXPLAIN
ADMIT
DENY
ASK WHY

Reversing

Reverse the objection by taking the reason the customer gives as the basis for their objection and turn it into a sales feature. If Mr Jones complains that continuous computer accounting forms you're selling are confusing, agree with him they might be a little difficult to understand at first, but they'll actually cut the time taken to check statements once staff become used to them. Impress on him that it's one of the best reasons for using your stationery.

Explaining

Explain Mr Jones's objection away with facts if it's founded on misunderstanding. Don't let him feel small if his objection was ill-founded. It's better for the sake of a sale to shoulder the responsibility for the misunderstanding by apologising for not having made things clearer earlier on. Then back this up by explaining all the benefits.

Admitting

Admit it if you're in the wrong or if the objection is a valid one. Once you've admitted the problem you will have let the heat out of the original objection. Tell Mr Jones you (or your company) were in error, then pause slightly before assuring him it won't happen again and the reasons why not.

Denying

Deny very courteously anything said about you, your company or the product which is untrue or unfair. Express pleasure at being able to scotch any rumours or false facts, then talk about more positive reasons for buying.

Asking why

Why – always ask why Mr Jones objects. By getting him to talk about his objection, he'll explain much of it away and at the same time reveal any related objections for you to answer.

So there we have the simple rules for overcoming objections and turning them to our advantage. There are two other techniques to perfect:

- *Change an objection into a question* – a particularly useful technique when faced with a price objection from the customer. You counter an objection on price from Mr Jones with something like: 'Have I got your question right? You want to know how to make more profit by using our services?' The original question on price has been converted to one nearer the buyer's heart – profit!
- *'Yes', followed by a pause.* This is the technique by which you agree that Mr Jones has a valid point, pause, then tell him of the features that will overcome the problem he has raised.

EXAMPLES OF OVERCOMING OBJECTIONS

Adopt the right attitude to sales resistance. A professional salesperson shouldn't fear objections but accept them as a fact of life and be prepared to combat them. Look upon objections as the customer's way of seeking to be more convinced and assured. And remember, the onus is on you to do the convincing – not the customer to convince themselves.

Price
This is the most important one to be overcome by the skilful salesperson. Why do customers often object to prices? Among the most likely reasons are:

- The customer hasn't the money.
- They haven't budgeted enough to pay as much.
- They assumed it would cost less.
- The price is being used as an excuse for some other reason.
- The customer has in mind the lower price of your competitor.
- An attempt on the customer's part to bargain.
- You have not convinced the customer on *value* and *benefits*.

First of all look critically at the way you've been selling your product or service. Can you honestly say, hand on heart, that you've been basing the sale on *value* and *benefits* rather than just price? Insufficient emphasis on benefits is the main reason behind the majority of objections to price. Always keep stressing those benefits.

Competitor's prices
Another common reason for price objection is where a competitor is involved. Here again it's important for you as the salesperson to keep the benefits of the product or service at the forefront throughout the discussion.

Disclosing the price
At what stage should the price be revealed? As a general rule, keep any mention of price as late as possible in the sales interview. Only when you've made the customer understand the full scope and value of the offer can they view price objectively in its right perspective. Every salesperson fears, quite understandably, the prospective buyer who asks 'How much?' too soon into the presentation. There's a real danger that a direct answer early on could disrupt the smooth running of a carefully planned sales interview or even kill your chances of a sale stone dead right at the outset.

Work out ways of putting off the answer, without causing irritation, offending the customer, appearing to evade the issue or being overly conscious and sensitive of the price. As a professional salesperson who doesn't try to sell the actual product or service, but concentrates instead on the benefits it offers, you must sell not on price but on *value*. Price then becomes a secondary consideration looked at in the proper perspective.

By fully stressing the amount of money to be saved or made by using your company's product or service in terms of increased productivity, profit, saving in time and space, say, you can make price appear to be less important. When you do mention the price, do it confidently and without any hesitation.

'Your product/service is too expensive'
Don't be put off by this claim from the customer. Overcoming this particular objection follows the usual pattern of a cushion enquiry (to establish if it's a component or the complete package the customer thinks is too expensive) that paves the way for subsequent questions:

* 'By how much?'

* 'Compared with what (or whom)?'

* Then: 'So if I could demonstrate ways in which financial aids like leasing or grants could be made available to reduce the initial capital outlay . . .'

Should the customer talk about the price being *way out of line*, it's an exaggeration that needs to be tackled by converting a price objection into a profit question:

* 'That's a fair enough comment, but let me get this right. What you're really saying is how can you make more profit by using our product/service, isn't it?'

You then go on the prove the points that add up to profit.

If a competitor is involved, the objection could be along the lines of 'Your price is much too dear' and when you ask why you're told: 'Compared with the price I'm paying with my present supplier.' Your answer is to agree that at first glance it could appear that way, then to point out to the customer:

- 'But have you considered (describe the benefits of your product or service) which you could use to increase your share of the market and end up with higher profit?'

Influence and pressure

These commonly feature in sales resistance and the ability to tackle them lies entirely with you. If you try to dominate the sales interview and aren't prepared to listen to the customer, the pressure will increase until something blows – probably your chances of making a sale!

Winning arguments often loses sales. It can't be emphasised enough: *listen* more instead of talking when a customer expresses objections. Develop the skill of *leading not pushing* the customer. It's vital to empathise with them and put yourself in their place. That way, you'll be well on the way to handling this particular sales resistance.

Variance

Here's another frequently raised objection. There will always be occasions when this objection can't be overcome. This is not being negative – it's a fact that we have to accept. An example is where there is a problem with the application of the product.

You'll find very often, though, that a customer raises the objection through not *fully understanding* the benefits of the proposition you're putting to them. It's most important you clarify the exact extent of the variance to the customer.

'Too busy now'

This is one of the objections we come across earlier on when discussing overcoming objections on the telephone. Very often, the customer invites you to leave some literature and promises to 'think about it'. In many cases, this is sheer prevarication – the customer is making these excuses to avoid having to make a decision on the spot.

There could be other, more hidden reasons behind this objection which you should endeavour to discover.

The person you're talking to isn't a budget holder
This person doesn't have the authority to buy. In this situation find out, diplomatically and with delicacy, who the right person is and make an appointment to see them. Even better would be to involve your present contact by asking them to take you to the right person. Make sure you don't belittle the person to whom you are speaking. Here's where the *you* word comes in useful: 'Whom else do *you* involve in decisions of this nature, Mr Jones?' strikes just the right note. To recap on what we've already learned about preparation, the 'authority to buy' problem can often be avoided by making a high level of contact right from the start. It's much easier to be 'passed down' in a firm than it is to be 'passed up'.

The customer is just trying to get you out of the door
Don't accept this and recapture their interest by the 'Yes', followed by a pause, technique: 'I realise you are busy, Mr Jones. Perhaps I can give you a little extra information so that you can make the decision now and get it out of the way.'

The customer really does want to study in depth what your company has to offer
Ask if you can come back and go over your proposal with them. Again, you can employ the 'Yes' pause technique as above.

An alternative technique is the 'Yes', pause, followed by positive suggestions:

• 'I fully understand, Mr Jones, that you are a busy man and that this is a big decision to make. Why not start using our product/service now so that when you come to make the final decision you'll have some to judge from?'

This strategy is also in keeping with the law of maximum and minimum objectives, i.e. to leave the room with all the business or at least some of it, whether it's an agreement, an action or a concession on the customer's part.

'I haven't time to see you'
A variation of the previous objection, this is a popular method of fobbing off a salesperson. It's a case of 'Yes', pause, then arrange a future appointment using the alternative closing technique. Always emphasise you'll be as brief as possible. Don't attempt to browbeat the customer into granting you a meeting. The more you insist, the

more the customer will dig their heels in and refuse to see you on this or indeed possibly on any future occasions.

Your company
'I don't like your company – it's too big'
Counter this with the 'Yes', pause technique, followed by an explanation:

- 'Yes, Mr Jones, I can see your point and realise how easy it is to get that impression, but it's not quite as straightforward as it might appear. Having started off in a small way ourselves, we are very supportive of private enterprise. In fact, we rely on hundreds of small manufacturers who own their own business. We couldn't do without them and, for their part, they find it better to deal with a single customer – my customer. They don't have the worries of invoicing, debt collecting or soliciting business. By dealing with us, you'll be supporting many little businesses as well.'

A bald statement like 'I don't like your company' should be queried with 'Why?' If it's because 'I like to give my business to the smaller concerns', again you can tell Mr Jones you can see his point of view, but tell him:

- 'By giving us your business, you are actually supporting hundreds of small businesses as well. The whole business world today is so competitive and complex that smaller concerns by themselves often can't keep up with the requirements of larger, more modern companies. You can make more profit by using our company's product. Let me show you how.'

Again, you're using the 'Yes' pause technique, followed by an explanation.

'Bad experience with your company'
Never fall into the trap of holding a post-mortem into the whys and wherefores. What's happened has happened. Convince the customer the same problems will not reoccur. Offer them an apology or deal with any outstanding query, keeping the conversation on current track. What are the customer's needs *now*?

'I've tried your people before and the product just didn't do what the salesperson claimed it would'
This objection lends itself to the 'Yes' pause technique, followed by an explanation. First find out how long it was since the customer tried

your company, then counter with:

- 'Four years ago? I'm sorry to hear that, Mr Jones. You've got a fairly large labour force in your plant, haven't you?'

When Mr Jones agrees that's so, follow up with 'So you find human error causes a few problems from time to time?' Another 'Yes' from the customer and you can continue with

- 'We're in exactly the same position. Human error causes us problems on occasions – not often, but it does happen. My company has state-of-the-art production facilities and a really good team. We're proud of our record and our products. Why not order a batch now? I promise you you'll see the problem you had was an isolated incident.'

If you know what the objection is and you know the product didn't do the job expected of it, then use the admit it technique, followed by positive suggestion:

- 'Yes, I accept that you did have some trouble with the product. But we've now ironed out the problems. If you place an order with us, you'll see just how good our product standards will be in the future.'

Your competitors
'We have other companies to see'
Your answer to this one should be, 'Naturally. Could I ask how many will be involved?' You then need to find out who they are, on what basis the customer will make their choice and when they'll be seeing the salespeople. You're now in the position to say, 'Good, so I can make an appointment to see you . . .'

'I don't know much about your company. Your competitors are much better known'
Don't be fazed by this rebuff. Tell the customer that it's quite understandable, then ask what companies they are used to dealing with. Give a brief description of your company, adding any testimonials from well-known organisations. Then, 'What details would you like further assurance on? So then, if . . . you'll feel much happier . . .'

'My first reaction is that another company has a better solution'
Your reply should be:

- 'I appreciate what you're saying. Which company is it? May I first check that both of us are looking at the project in hand with the same brief?'

Gently pin the customer down to the particular area they're concerned about, which area is different, and how the rival company has tackled a certain topic. Then you come in with 'So if . . .' which, it has already been stressed, is a most useful questioning device.

You

'I'm not yet convinced'
Step in quickly with the cushion statement: 'Of course, I've yet to tell you more about us.' Then go on to summarise the company's background and the benefits its products offer the customer. Subsequent questions could enquire what further benefits the customer is looking for or what parts they don't understand or are troubled about. Then our familiar device comes into play: 'So if I can . . .'

'I don't like you!'
This begs an instant 'Why?' from you, followed by you explaining the facts and accepting the criticism with courtesy. If the customer dislikes you 'because you're too young and aggressive', tell them you're sorry if your enthusiasm gave the impression of your being aggressive. Then explain how your eagerness and enthusiasm sometimes runs away from you. Although this objection is reasonably rare, it can be raised. Whatever you do, always avoid giving offence to the customer.

'I don't think your proposition is good enough'
You will of course, want to know why. 'That's a fair comment, Mr Jones. What do I have to do to get your business?'

Time

'I have the idea, but the time isn't right'
The cushion reply is:

* 'Fine, that's good, so it's only a question of time, Mr Jones?' or
* 'So if we forget about the time for the moment, how happy are you otherwise with the concept of . . . ?'

Your subsequent questions will be regarding the factors that influence the timing and what needs to happen between the present and you and the customer getting together again for a further meeting. ('So if we were to set the time for a further meeting on . . . how would that fit in?')
'It's the wrong time for us to buy'

This could be a genuine objection, but it can also be a fob-off. You'll need to investigate very thoroughly the reasons for any delay in decision-making.

'I'll think it over'
Beware particularly of this 'assurance'. It's perhaps the most hackneyed method of getting rid of salespeople. Wherever possible employ the 'special inducement' close.

The customer's colleagues
'I would like to discuss it with colleagues first'
Your cushion reply is to ask the names and the titles of the colleagues involved. You'll also want to probe further and get an idea of their likely views and reaction regarding your product. How will the customer decide whether or not to go ahead? 'If it were your decision alone, Mr Jones, how happy would you be to go ahead?' should give you a good idea as to the way things will go. The subsequent question is: 'What haven't I told you that you need to know?' The next cushion question concerns how soon it will be before the customer gets to confer with colleagues, followed by you expressing your willingness to help with any further information. Then clinch the next meeting with 'so, let's pencil in a date in our diaries. How about . . . or perhaps . . . ?'

'I'm convinced, but I can't see my board/boss giving me the go-ahead'
Share the customer's disappointment with the cushion remark:

* 'Oh, that would be a pity! What reservations do you think they might have?' and follow with

* 'So if we could arrange a presentation for your board/boss, do you think that might help?

Current suppliers
'You haven't persuaded me to change from my current supplier'
Loyalty to an existing supplier might manifest itself in a customer's comment. Your follow-up questions could be either

* 'How long have you been with your current supplier? or
* 'What attracted you to them in the first place?' followed by
* 'So if I can demonstrate that my product has the benefit of being better, cheaper . . . etc.' and
* 'which of my company's benefits I've mentioned so far are of interest to you?'

Of you could ask the direct question: 'What would make you change your supplier?'

PROVING YOUR CASE

No matter how professional your sales presentation skills, you'll often find it necessary to prove to the customer the benefits you have to offer. Proof can be introduced during the sales interview to:

• Gain and hold attention.
• Create interest.
• Create benefit selling opportunities.
• Support a claim or a benefit you've sold.
• Help overcome objections or complaints.
• Get decisions.
• Aid selling to the person with authority to buy absent from the actual interview.
• Create closing signals (watch the customer for visual signals showing they're ready to make a decision).

> **Absence of proof – or the wrong proof – can be detrimental to your selling efforts. Sometimes it results in objections.**

Using proof
It will be part of your preplanning to decide before any meeting whether you'll need proof to ensure your presentation is

• more credible
• more understandable
• memorable and registers.

Types of proof
Physical proof is provided by samples or visits organised by you to enable prospective customers to see your showroom, factory or warehouse for themselves. We'll look at this in more detail.

Case history proof takes the form of a factual report provided by you on a sale to a similar company as that of the prospect. It gives details of performance, savings, general comments and other relevant details.

News and reports, literature, testimonials, price lists, proposals, independent surveys and design work are all *visual proof* for the customer to study.

Showroom or factory visits

Such visits can make a good impression on the customer if well organised. They are, however, time consuming and expensive. Therefore before going ahead with any visit, you must first decide it is a necessary step towards your goal – a favourable decision from the customer. The timing of the visit is particularly vital and the sale can be lost if this is wrong. A visit should be arranged to fit into the decision-making process so as to achieve the following aims:

- Help take the case to a higher person with authority to buy where necessary.
- Clinch the order.
- Get money set aside specifically in the budget.
- Eliminate any competition.

Unless these aims are not achievable during a visit, then you can count on it being the wrong time or for the wrong reasons.

Necessary criteria for a visit

Organise a visit only when some or all of the persons from the targeted company cannot be persuaded to decide in your company's favour without seeing the showroom or factory. So, therefore, of the situations which follow, one or a combination of them must exist:

- The need for your product or service still has to be proved to some or all of the prospective customers.

- The benefits and advantages over their present methods your company offers have to be proved.

- The system has to be seen first hand so they can see it answers their needs.

- Your benefits over those of competitors have to be proved.

- Benefits must be seen to justify the financial outlay.

- Quality has to be proved.

- Specification requirements are outside the norm.

- The size, operation and dependability of your company needs to be proved.

When arranging a visit, keep the following in mind:

- You must have a very clear picture of who the people are you will be showing around. Make sure that all those involved in decision-making who need to see the proof will be present.

- Ensure everyone attending is briefed on the location and timing of the visit. And don't forget to make clear what they do on arrival. Do they report to security or reception? Or, better still, will you be on hand to greet them personally?

- When it entails a showroom visit, ensure this has been entered in the office diary and that all the members of your company's team who should be on hand have been informed and will be available.

- Right at the start of the visit the situation as it stands should be reviewed. Employ agreement-seeking questions to establish you're aware of the prospective customer's needs and are about to show them the solution.

- Before starting the product presentation, make a statement of intention detailing what you intend to demonstrate and why.

- Whatever you do, avoid the kind of product presentation containing a list of meaningless features. Choose only those which you can convert into benefits.

- As soon as you've finished the presentation, use agreement-seeking questions again to make sure you've covered all points, the benefits have been made clear to your listeners and that they've accepted the proof offered.

Which site?

Often a prospective customer will want to see your product in operation at an existing user's office or factory. When organising such a visit, consider these questions carefully:

- Are the user's needs applicable to those of your prospective customer?

- Is the complete range of your company's products being used? It could be embarrassing to you if the prospective customer's team spot one of your competitor's products in use. It's likely to put doubts in their minds!

- Is the existing user likely to have any outstanding queries or complaints? If so, these must be sorted out well in advance.

- Is the timing right, or will the visit led by you cause problems?

- Can you be sure the product will be shown at its best?

OUT-COMPETING THE COMPETITION

Whatever our particular field in the realm of sales, we have to accept that the market is increasingly competitive and is likely to remain so in the foreseeable future. But it's wrong to assume that competition is always there. Salespeople often make a rod for their own backs by actually prompting customers to approach other suppliers. Questions like 'What other products have you been looking at?' get the customers thinking that perhaps they ought to be looking elsewhere and making comparisons.

One of your responsibilities as a professional salesperson is to provide your management with good market intelligence. This means collecting information about all existing competitors and other competition likely to arise. This will help your management in the planning of future strategy and product development.

Never undersell yourself or underestimate the important part you play at the sharp end. You are the professional in everything you set out to do for yourself and your company. Competition is a challenge not a threat. No matter how strong your competitors are in a given situation, unless they get the timing right and sell real benefits to real prospective customers they will not pose a serious threat.

Learn all you can about your competitors' strengths and weaknesses. Listen to the comments of users of their products and study their literature. This will enable you to select benefit areas unique to your product and to handle each situation separately. Look upon competitors with healthy respect by all means, but never let the competition worry you.

Evasion not attack

In active combat the best means of defence might well be attack, but avoidance is better when it comes to sales competition. Sound pre-planning and good investigation on your first contact will enable you to do make a good sales pitch at the first interview with a prospective customer. The prospect will then be less likely to start looking elsewhere.

Capture the prospect's attention and interest from the outset. Maintain the initiative with a close eye on the timescale involved, so you're in a position to deliver the goods when the moment arrives. This will ensure the prospect won't consider alternative sources because of apparent disinterest on your part.

Never, ever, introduce competitors by name into the conversation – or for that matter imply a product equivalent or similar to your own exists. And when you do clinch the sale, make sure the customer

– once they become an existing user – gets the best possible sales service. Again, this will make sure they have no cause to go elsewhere. Don't rest on your laurels. Existing business is not yours by right and customers you've gained after a great deal of effort can easily be lost by complacency.

Meeting competition

Never run the competition down but, at the same time, don't praise competitors too much to a prospective or existing customer. If a competing company is introduced into the conversation, just pay your competitor a vague but brief compliment before returning as soon as possible to discussing the benefits you have to offer. You can, of course, seize the opportunity to select relevant benefits (adjusting these where necessary) and stress the advantages of your company's product over that of your competitor.

Even if you feel worried, don't show it. And if the customer has introduced a competitor's name to raise a price objection, remember to convert this in terms of a cost difference and handle it accordingly.

If you find yourself quoting on price against a cheaper competitor, ensure your proposal includes a review of the current situation and stresses all the benefits to the customer. This is particularly necessary where the person with authority to buy is not present and might have to base their decision on information passed on to them second-hand. Without the benefits being fully explained, they will tend to favour the lowest price.

As with all sales interviews and presentations, always establish the prospective customer's buying motives and keep them clearly in mind

---

HOLDING THE INITIATIVE

More sales are lost through the seller failing to hold on to the initiative than for any other reason. If you know you're on to a cert with a particular prospective customer, your next job is to work out how to keep control of the selling situation through all stages. Remember it's not only for this order, but for future business.

Let's be realistic. There aren't enough hours in the working day to enable you to keep track of all your prospects' timesales. This means you must decide on priorities and it's important that large potential prospects and new business and competitive situations must be at the top of your list. Use the telephone wherever possible to maintain close contact.

Some guidelines
Prospective customers
It's essential to establish the full potential of any prospective customer when making your pre-investigation call or at the very latest on your first selling call. You need to be sure, too, that the person or persons you contact will have authority to make the decision in your favour. Your knowledge must be complete as possible.

Timescale
If you're to crystallise your aims and objectives, you must thoroughly investigate the timescale involved. The knowledge gained will enable you to plan how to hold the initiative from start to finish and keep the momentum going. Don't assume without being told, or accept vague answers regarding tender dates, purchasing schedules and delivery times. Ensure you know the exact dates of meetings within the prospect's organisation at which decisions affecting you will be made. Make sure, too, you and the prospect are aware of decision dates with a view to delivery. Check and confirm that people in the prospect's organisation are available and that they

* want it
* need it
* are able to receive it.

While it is important that everything fits in with your plans to suit you, make sure you can meet the prospect's timescale and don't allow the competition to gain a toehold.

Modifying your aims
While you must always keep your aims and objectives in mind and work to a plan, these are by no means cast in stone. Always retain a degree of flexibility, because there will come a time where you have to make changes or amendments. When this occurs, make sure you still have the initiative by:

* Fixing the next appointment to suit the timescale.
* Agreeing the action with the customer and your follow-up.
* Agreeing on a decision time, together with your follow-up.

> **Only amend your aims and objectives when it becomes absolutely necessary.**

An air of efficiency

Maintain an air of efficiency and the prospective customer will be more likely to let you take the initiative and make the running. Ways of adding to your reputation for efficiency and professionalism are:

- Listening attentively and intelligently.

- Taking notes throughout a meeting, particularly of promises made, complaints, delivery dates and technical data.

- Giving an update of the current situation to give the prospect confidence you have understood their needs.

- Frequently using you diary to show you are organised and have a well planned and busy schedule.

Delaying tactics

Perhaps one of the most frequent statements made by prospects to delay making a decision is: 'You'll have to leave it with me for the moment.' If this happens you're in danger of losing the initiative, so apply the following criteria:

- Confirm the reason for the delay.

- If it's valid, agree the date of the next meeting or action to be taken to fit in with the timescale.

- If the reason's not genuine, major on selling the benefits to the prospect of making a decision now.

When the delay is due to the absence of the person who has the authority to make a decision and the power to purchase, follow these sequences:

1. If the prospect says they'll have to have a word with the person concerned, your reaction will be 'Fine, let's see Mr Jones now!' or 'When's Mr Jones likely to be back?'

If, on the other hand, it's not possible to see Mr Jones right at that moment:

2. 'It would be a good idea if we saw him together, wouldn't it? When do you suggest? Or 'When will you be seeing Mr Jones?'

If (1) is ruled out, make sure your contact is well briefed to put the case for buying with enough literature, technical data and a proposal prepared by you detailing all the benefits. Give them the telephone number of a suitable contact in your office in case of difficulties or queries arising at the meeting. A telephone call from you on the day before the meeting to finalise details will help bolster up the confidence of the contact putting the case for buying before the person with authority.

Finally, get the contact to agree on a date and time for a follow-up telephone call from you to get a decision. If the prospect asks you to 'Leave it with me and I'll give you a ring', regain the initiative along the lines of 'I'm rather difficult to get hold of at the moment. You'll know by next Tuesday, won't you? I'll give you a ring on Wednesday morning them'.

Avoiding decision delays

Confirm your prospect's timescale *before* you talk about delivery or the next action date. That way you'll avoid creating a decision delay. If, in answer to a question from the prospect, you give them delivery details straight away, they're likely to sit back and relax because they've plenty of time. They could, of course, think such a delivery schedule is out of the question and mentally discount you and your product.

The right answer to the question, 'What's your delivery at the moment?', is 'When do you need it, Mr Jones?' When Mr Jones tells you he wants it, say, by the 10th of next month at the latest, you ask if you can use his phone to ring through the order. Better still, if you've already made yourself familiar with the prospect's timescale, you can tell him: 'I believe you mentioned the 10th of next month for delivery, Mr Jones. If we can just complete the paperwork now, I'll ensure it's on time. Could I have an order number, please?'

Sales literature and quotations

No matter how attractively designed, well written and illustrated your sales literature, it won't help you keep the momentum going on its own. Don't just leave it with a prospect in the hope it will achieve great things. Its true worth is as an aid to your sales presentation.

Should the quotation be by way of an official confirmation, receipt of which will signal the time of an order, strike while the iron's hot. Call in with it and take the order. If, however, the quotation is prepared as a stage in the sales operation, make sure it is a proposal detailing, in précis form on a separate attached sheet, all the benefits. Check and make sure any quotation or proposal fits in with the timescale.

Planning for the future

One of your objectives, especially when making an information call or indeed at any stage in the sales process before securing an order, must always be to look ahead and make sure of the next call. To sell this to the customer, you've always got to have some justifiable reason for calling again, such as:

* new products in the pipeline
* future applications
* expansion plans
* an introduction to a prospect's colleague.

Keep up to date with the situation by using the telephone. Don't forget to note telephone contact dates in your diary.

Obtain agreement to the next stages, always keeping firmly in the driving seat. For instance, if Mr Jones tells you nothing's going to happen before July, tell him you'll give him a ring in the mean time to make sure nothing has changed. Add that you'll be in his area in July and suggest dates that would be mutually convenient.

HANDLING ABSENT AUTHORITIES

There are bound to be occasions when you'll find that one or more of the prospective customers you plan to sell to – those with the authority to buy – are unavailable or inaccessible. Before you go any further, make absolutely sure there's no possibility of getting together with them; that it's not a fob-off or intervention by a zealous or over-protective member of staff. Don't accept the situation of selling through third parties readily. Always offer to accompany your contact to the meeting.

If you find there's no way round the situation, bear in mind you've got to pitch your sales presentation with the absent authority in mind. Although it's necessary to retain the attention and interest of your initial contact, you must also ensure you're making a case that will appeal to the buying motives of the absent person or persons.

Money, authority, need (MAN) and timescale

First of all do some thorough detective work and investigate the person who has control of the budget and the authority to purchase. Also find out who is likely to influence the authority absent from your discussions. As always, you must establish what timescale is involved. On any subsequent call you make, check nothing has changed. Like all things, the more complete your understanding of a particular company's set-up, its people who do the actual buying and the timescale envisaged, the better. You'll be able to decide on whom to call and when, so as to get decisions.

As part of what you've discovered, you'll be clear in your mind as to:

- Which person will sell to the absent authority in your stead.
- What type of case will you need to prepare in writing for a meeting.
- What kind of proposal is to be made to the individual concerned.

Your contact is not likely to be a sales or marketing person. You can't expect them to do a really good selling job for you unless they're armed with a carefully prepared and targeted brief from you. The contact will probably only get as far as discussing the features of your product or service which, without the benefits being explained, could sound expensive. Sales literature that has not been specially selected or prepared will only make the situation worse. No, you must give your contact something much more than just sales material and a price list.

Skilful questioning will also elicit from your contact what sort of person or persons you are dealing with through a third party. You must learn how the absent authority is likely to see the need, authority, spending of money and timescale situation, so that you can work out their buying motives.

Prepare questions such as:

- How do they usually make decisions of this kind?
- How much do they get involved in budgets?
- What are the plans for future expansion?
- What do they know of your problems?
- What don't they like about . . . ?
- Whom do they usually discuss things with before making a decision?

Establish these details:

- The date of the meeting.
- The people who will be attending.
- Whether they've already been informed about what you are offering.
- If the meeting is formal or informal.

Offer to help your contact with any writing of reports or specifications, and brief them thoroughly with:

- your objectives
- suitably marked-up sales literature
- visual aids.

Get in touch with your contact just prior to the meeting to go over further details. Make sure they know how to get in touch with you during the meeting if queries arise or there's a need for clarification. And ensure you'll be available for consultation on the day.

Although physically absent, you're hoping someone is going to do the job for you, so make sure your contact themselves are enthusiastic and sold on the idea. If need be, become something of a sales coach yourself!

Group selling

You could, however, find your presence is required by a group or board of people who have joint responsibility and authority for purchasing. This requires you to carry out good pre-investigation so that you know:

- The date of the meeting.

- The venue.

- Names, positions and titles of the people who will attend and the pecking order.

- Who are the actual decision-makers.

- And the stages the decision-making progress has to go through.

First get your contact 'sold', then brief them thoroughly – you may need their help. Decide on your objectives and treat the occasion as a normal presentation. Prepare a seating plan, if possible, and get to the venue early to put out the name cards and introduce yourself to your audience as they enter the room.

As this is rather like public speaking, prepare notes for your presentation and handouts. Make sure you have sufficient so that everyone present has one and isn't reduced to sharing – if they don't know, they could say 'No' to your proposals. Employ visuals, too, but make sure they can be seen.

Don't get involved in detailed discussion with one particular person. But by all means get everyone to take part with the use of questions and positive suggestions, so that it's not a monologue on your part. Just telling 'em is not selling to 'em. Get your listeners actively involved. Where those present cannot come to overall unanimous agreement, determine those parts they do agree on and get agreement in stages.

Throughout the presentation remember it will be your general manner, bearing and way of speaking which will have an effect on how your message is received. Above all, demonstrate sound knowledge of your product or service.

TO SUM UP

Handing objections

Objections, while taking many and varied forms, will basically be one of three types. There are sincere (valid) ones or insincere (invalid) ones designed to fob you off. We've also mentioned hidden objections, where a prospect is unwilling to accept a point that will implicate them with regard to the sale, so they put forward an objection or a 'stalling' comment which masks the true objection.

Correctly handling an objection is not an end in itself, but serves to bring you one step nearer an objective – either agreement or the order. When you've answered the objection to the satisfaction of the buyer, press home the advantage by either attempting to close or getting back on track towards your objective.

Overcoming common objections

Remember the mnemonic – READY – **R**everse, **E**xplain, **A**dmit, **D**eny, ask wh**Y**. Adopt the right attitude to sales resistance – don't fear objections but accept them as a fact of life. Regard objections as the customer's way of seeking reassurance.

Proving your case

No proof or the wrong proof can result in objections. Arrange visits to your factory or showroom, or to the premises of a customer already using your product, with great care.

Out-competing the competition

Studying your competitors carefully will mean you can pinpoint the benefits of your own products. Don't run your competitors down and don't panic if a competitor's lower price is introduced as an objection – re-emphasise the benefits of your own product.

Holding the initiative

Establish clear timescales with your prospects so that you maintain control of the situation and prevent the competition from gaining a toehold. However, be flexible, retain an air of efficiency and deal with delaying tactics effectively. Always keep an eye on the future – so you have good reason to contact a prospect or customer again.

Handling absent authorities

If the person you are selling to is not the person with the authority to buy, tease out as much information about the absent authority from the person you are dealing with as possible. If a meeting is planned with the absent authority/authorities, use your contact again to glean as much information as you can about who will attend, details of the meeting, etc. If the contact is holding the meeting in your stead, ensure they are briefed to the best of your ability and that they can contact you should the need arise. In a group selling situation, prepare your presentation thoroughly in advance.

9

Negotiation

SELLING VERSUS NEGOTIATION

Selling began from the moment people starting communicating their ideas to others with their first grunts. In fact it's been labelled by the more cynical among us as the world's second oldest profession. But one thing is certain. Through the ages, the caveman flogging animal skins, the Phoenician trading with the Ancient Britons, the itinerant vendor doing the rounds of local fairs and you, the professional salesperson of today, all have one thing in common – an ability to communicate with the customers. No matter how good your product or service, you won't sell successfully without being able to let prospective buyers know it exists, that it's the best thing since sliced bread and that it will meet their needs.

Selling comes first

Selling always comes before *negotiation*. The simple difference between them is the timing. With selling you tell people what you've got, what it's going to do for them and how much it costs. If they don't like it, the sale is unsuccessful; if they like it and buy it, you've achieved a successful sale. Negotiation follows when prospective customers like what they see, but want to haggle about the price. If you and they can't reach an agreement, negotiation has been unsuccessful; likewise if you do come to an agreement, the outcome is a successful negotiation.

So negotiation begins when the prospect wants to buy and you want to sell, but you still have a few details to thrash out regarding terms and conditions. Negotiation is playing an ever-increasing role in the commercial world. The supplier and buyer relationship, which was traditionally viewed as a selling one, has changed considerably over the last decade or so. Many major customers have developed their own business strategies that are just as sophisticated as those of the major manufacturers. There is an appreciable growing concentration of buying power in fewer hands.

This obviously has significance for all salespeople, so it's worth while looking more closely at the trend. First, instead of a product being spread around, an increasing percentage of the output of suppliers is being purchased by a few individuals who have considerable power and buying authority. Again, at the same time both suppliers and customers are developing their own individual hierarchies of salespeople and purchasers:

Supplier	*Customer*
Senior account manager	Buying director
Account manager	Regional buyer
Account executive	Buyer
Salesperson	Branch manager

Because many customers are now passing responsibility for profits down the line, this frequently means all the supplier's representatives (senior account manager *et al.*) have to:

- *Sell* the product or service individually before it actually reaches the user; that is, right down the customer's line (from the buying director downwards, 'authority' takes the form of a listing indicating to the person below they can buy if they wish).

- *Negotiate* the terms and conditions individually under which their product or service will eventually reach the user.

So it's becoming increasingly important now for sales representatives, whatever their title, to be both skilful salespeople and negotiators. They also need matching confidence and self-esteem, for there are various reasons why a salesperson might be anxious to sell, perhaps giving the customer the impression of being too desperate, such as:

- Statistically, individual customers are more important – they know it and so does the salesperson.

- In a highly competitive situation the salesperson is aware suppliers who aren't already doing business with the customer will attempt to 'buy' their way in.

- Competition between customers will result in them beating down the supplier on price to give them the advantage over their competitors.

On a more personal level, the salesperson will be conscious that:

- Size, bureaucracy and computers erode the personal nature of buying.

- There is immense pressure on every salesperson down the supplier's line not to be the one to break the negotiating chain.

- Fewer salespeople are needed, so individuals feel a certain lack of security.

So we're left with a situation whereby both buyer and salesperson – often both without being aware of it – could encourage the seller to assume the role of *the poor man at the rich man's gate.*

The nature of selling
If we examine a typical sales interview with seller and buyer interacting with one another, we get an insight into both parties' needs.
 The salesperson's needs will be revealed by their

- opening statement
- presentation of product features and benefits
- close of the sale.

The customer will show their needs by

- questions
- attitude and personality
- objections
- agreement.

The objective of the seller is to concentrate on raising the buyer's need (as perceived by the buyer) for the product or service to a level where, to satisfy that need, the customer makes a decision to buy. In selling, the salesperson maintains their position while persuading the buyer to move towards them by heightening the buyer's perception of their need for the product or service. We've already seen how this is done by selling the *benefits,* at the price quoted. The customer, made aware of their need for the product or service, is brought to the point where it's irresistibly available to them.

The buyer is induced to make all the running by the salesperson's selling technique which embodies simple objectives and accompanying criteria for success.

Leading to negotiation
The customer has moved to a position where, to satisfy their heightened perception of need, they have to consider the necessary buying decision. Successful sales technique is not negotiation, but the basis on which negotiation can now take place.
 The customer, having been satisfied during the selling process it is

OK to go ahead and actively consider buying, will now seek to get the best possible deal in a number of areas. The customer will discuss the terms and conditions connected with the sale and purchase:

- *Price* – the buyer will want to go into discounts, bonuses, savings or losses and when and how payment is to be made.

- *Product* – details of packaging, range or mix, precise specification will be requested.

- *Service* – the buyer will question the seller on delivery (when and where) and reliability, finance and credit, technical support and servicing, promotional support, and training for staff.

This is where negotiation really begins, based on a common need to buy and supply created by selling, and final terms and conditions surrounding the decision to purchase and supply are hammered out. In the negotiation phase of the sales process the supplier assumes the mantle of the negotiator and takes the detail of the marketing mix of product, price and presentation and tailors it to fit the local and immediate needs of the particular customer of the moment.

Both supplier and buyer become involved in what is known as controlled compromise, which experienced negotiators recognise and accept. It often clashes with the essentially uncompromising nature of the sales process and is in a way alien to a salesperson. The negotiator has more to do than a salesperson. In their interaction with buyers not only do they have to do everything the salesperson does – they then must have the skills to negotiate a mutually satisfying and successful outcome. The negotiator's job is not so much a different one from the salesperson's, but rather in the nature of an extra one on top of sales.

So whatever a person's position or title in the supplier's structure (i.e. account manager or account executive), they have to recognise they are, first and foremost, a salesperson. Without a salesperson's skills in judging needs, selling benefits and staging effective presentations, either:

- They won't have anything to negotiate, because they'll have been shown the door early on.

- Or their lack-lustre sales presentation means they've a much tougher negotiation on their hands.

The better the sales presentation, the higher the buyer's level of perceived need to buy. It's the difference between the buyer telling you 'It's not really what we're looking for, but I might consider it if you can offer me a good deal' and 'Yes, it's just the job! How quickly could we have some? Is the price negotiable?'

> **So the message is loud and clear: if you want to be a successful negotiator, develop your sales skills first**.

The biggest difference between the salesperson proper and the negotiator who combines sales skills with those of negotiation is that the latter usually has fewer customers. This is because the negotiator has an extra job to do and has the kind of customer high in the chain of command, perhaps even the major buyer at head office.

Is it negotiating – or dealing with objections?

The salesperson presents the product at a price. Perhaps the customer isn't sure whether to buy or not or is hesitant about the amount to buy. Using their technique, the salesperson reassures the customer and gets a positive response. In other words, the objection has been handled successfully.

In some cases the customer will have valid reasons for not taking a large amount. Perhaps there truly isn't the storage space, or under 'in-house' accounting the customer's charged for the amount of products in stock. There could be an imminent stock check to complicate things. The salesperson has a change of handling the objection by raising the customer's perceived value of the package offered with, for example: 'I can only hold this special price for you for three days.' But if this fails, the salesperson has to negotiate.

In the next section we'll cover negotiating techniques more fully, but there's one rule to take to heart right now, and that is:

> **A salesperson never gives anything away without getting something in return**.

A salesperson who readily accedes to a customer's request to split the delivery, for example, is going about things the wrong way. An astute seller, while sympathetic to the request, would bargain – perhaps by getting the customer to take an extra line in a promotion, for instance – before actually agreeing to split the delivery.

But, of course, it isn't all that easy. The customer could have valid reasons, but might not always express them. Such comments as:

- 'I'm unable to take that many at present'
- 'No, that's definitely too many to take at one time' or
- 'It wouldn't be worth me taking that many'

are signals from the customer (who might well be completely unaware they're making them) that they have valid reasons and want to negotiate.

The professional salesperson, positive in attitude and a good listener, will pick up on these signals, sympathise and follow them up: 'I suppose it does seem a lot. Is there any particular reason for your concern?' Hopefully this will encourage the customer to express their reasons and enable the salesperson either to negotiate or handle the objection in the usual way as necessary.

Different job functions

The salesperson's job could well progressively entail more negotiating and account management. This could come about gradually, accidentally, through promotion or as the result of restructuring. As and when the salesperson's job develops in this way, they must consciously acquire the additional skills required. Here are some of the main differences:

Selling – the salesperson
- Frequent calls.
  Strict journey planning
  Regular orders.
  Merchandising.
- Targeted to turnover and volume.
  Measured by calls, size of orders, strike rate, volume v. targets.
- Similarity between calls – the structure call.
- Strict selling policies – price, promotions, products against listings, etc.
- Buyers are similarly product and volume orientated.

Negotiating – the salesperson **and** *negotiator*
- Flexible and varied calls
  Decision-making approach to planning.
  Few orders.
  Delegates.
- Judged against forecasts and *profit* listings, account development, promotions and *statistics*.
- All calls planned individually.
- Negotiates conditions of sale for *profits* within company selling policies.
- Buyers are professional.

How the selling and negotiating processes differ from each other can be seen in Figure 9.

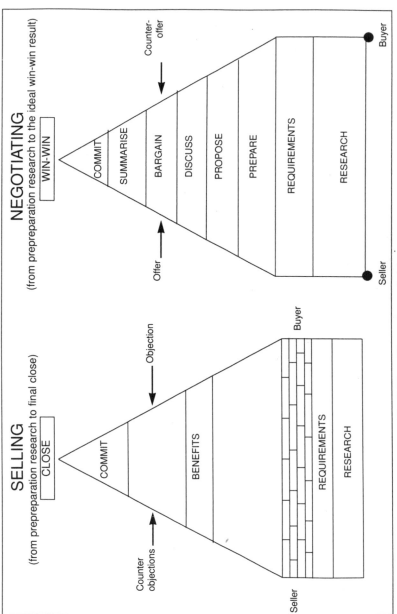

Fig. 9 The selling and negotiating processes.

THE ART OF NEGOTIATING

Negotiating has been defined as:

- A discussion between two sides, each with something to offer the other, on the terms and conditions of an exchange, with the objective that the resultant exchange is of benefit to both parties.

From our point of view, we can assume in this definition that some form of 'selling' has taken place. On the table between seller and buyer is a proposal, quotation, tender or a plan of some sort and both sides have agreed they're interested – provided terms and conditions can be agreed to their mutual satisfaction.

Perhaps the salesperson has just made a sales presentation and 'sold' the customer on the product or service. From initial disinterest to interest in the proposition, the buyer is now querying such details as price, volume, time scale for delivery and terms of payment. Or perhaps an account manager on behalf of the supplier is seeing a professional buyer with a detailed proposal formulated along a long series of meetings. In even simpler terms, it could be a builder submitting a quotation to a householder who wants an extra room created in the loft.

In all these hypothetical cases a point has been reached where both sides are seeking a satisfactory outcome from the discussions that will take place. The ideal outcome is a 'win-win' situation, where both parties see themselves better off than they were when negotiation started. But often the result is 'win-lose', 'lose-win' or 'lose-lose'.

Who is responsible for achieving the 'everyone's a winner' result? Obviously it would be marvellous if both parties shared equal responsibility for achieving this, but let's assume the responsibility is yours as the seller, and that the prospective customer is showing some reaction to what you're proposing but isn't consciously thinking about the negotiating process.

The psychological aspect
Perception and satisfaction
Perception and satisfaction, words, we've already used, imply that obtaining a good deal is not just down to facts and statistics. Looking at it simply, if we've beaten someone down from the first price they quoted for an item, we might be well pleased and slap ourselves on the back – that is, until we discover later another person got it for even less, of course! We experience a variety of feelings – of being superior, powerful or successful, or of having really achieved something. There will be others we might not even be conscious of, but in the end all feelings do control our *reactions*. So, as salespeople we

will try to control our own feelings while manipulating those of our customer. But we can only do this if we are aware of the various *sources* of those feelings influencing the customer's reaction.

The relationship between seller and customer
Although not analysed much this relationship probably exerts one of the strongest influences of all. You'll meet customers who'll want to do you down because they dislike you; others who like you and won't be able to do enough for you.

We've covered the most obvious ways by which you can alienate a customer, including boring the customer, irritating them, frustrating them by being indecisive, talking down to them. This creates a negative reaction on the customer's part. But, in the words of the old song, you've got to accentuate the positive and eliminate the negative. How? By flattering, consulting, even amusing the customer.

> **The important point to remember is: one way or another, the customer will be influenced by your behaviour.**

Your company
We've seen before, too, how a customer's impressions and prejudices, based on personal experience, gossip or hearsay, can have a bearing on how they react. If they think your company has a reputation for being unreliable, with representatives lacking in expertise and knowledge, they will be adversely influenced. On the other hand, if your company's name is synonymous in the customer's mind with reliability, quality, expertise and an excellent aftersales service, this can only go in your favour.

The proposition itself
This also has to be taken seriously into consideration. Does what you're offering strike the customer as exciting or prestigious or risky and possibly damaging to their career? Or is it so dull the customer couldn't care about things either way?

Pressures on the customer
The business environment of the customer poses many influences, such as pressure from above or below, constantly having to make the right decisions, interference from others or, quite simply, how content the customer is in their job.

As a professional salesperson cum negotiator you're already aware of such influences and try to steer the customer so that their reactions are increasingly positive to all the details and conditions under discussion. That way you are in the position to negotiate a good deal for yourself and one the customer is pleased with in terms of value satisfaction and the feel-good factor – in other words the ideal 'win-win' result.

The rules of making concessions

1. First be clear in your mind what you would like to get out of the negotiations; in other words, your personal aspirations. If you set your sights high, you'll usually get more. At the same time, you have to lower the other person's level of aspiration and make them ask for less. You can do this by exaggerating the gap in value between what you are offering and what is on offer in return. Beware of opening negotiation at too high an aspiration level on your part, as this could result in rejection and a breakdown in negotiations.

2. Most things in life are a question of 'give and take', but when it comes to concessions, you don't just *give* them, you *trade* them.

3. From the start think carefully what you want and what the other party wants, then ask yourself:

   - What concessions does your company usually give and *what are they worth* as far as the buyer's concerned?

   - What do you receive in return?

   - What concessions cost you little and are of value to the buyer?

   - Conversely, what concessions are of value to you and cheap to the buyer?

4. If you're going to make a concession, you must raise its *value* in the eyes of the other person. Maximise this to the full by

   - raising the *apparent cost* to you and

   - emphasising the *benefit* (that magic word again) your concession will provide them with.

5. Now *reduce the value of their concession* by telling them that it will

   - reduce the cost to them

   - reduce the benefit to you.

6. Trade concessions with reluctance. Don't give in easily. You've got to be mean – a little like Scrooge. It's a fact of life that every-

body puts greater value on things that are hard to get. The buyer will think they've reached the bottom line in the negotiations, but just before that deadline is reached, concede a little bit more.

7. Always endeavour to discover the buyer's workload. If they're busy, they'll settle more quickly, which means you can demand more in exchange.

8. However important concessions may be, always ensure you convince the buyer your company's product or service is right for them.

9. Keep in mind the deal as a whole and plan your strategy accordingly. If there are several points requiring negotiation, include them all before the bargaining begins.

10. Should the worse happen and negotiations become deadlocked, you'll then have to lower your sights and reduce your aspirations. But point out to the other party the time and trouble you have both invested and suggest another look before giving up entirely.

How buyers behave
As professional salespeople we have to be prepared for the tactics and countermeasures buyers employ before and during negotiations:

- The buyer likes your proposal, but finance is a problem.

  That's good to hear, but with a limited budget do you give a concession or offer an alternative? The buyer's going to win either way, let's face it, but always be prepared with alternatives. There's a good chance you can redeem the situation with an alternative that can still be profitable. For instance, suggest two-thirds down now and the remaining third later when the buyer has more money.

- The buyer puts you on the defensive by telling you you've got to come up with a better deal.

  Be ready to defend the price of your product or service and it's value to the buyer. If that doesn't work, trade a concession, which you've already had up your sleeve, for a close of sale. Other answers would be to design some form of 'inflation' in the price or speed up the terms of the deal.

- The buyer agrees in principle, then allows time to pass – lowering your aspirations – before coming back and wanting more or to take something back.

  This ploy is hard to resist. To counter it you first need to be aware of what's happening, then call the buyer's bluff. When the buyer comes back with stiffer terms, escalate the terms of the deal, taking something back or raising the price, then let the buyer screw you down to the original level. This prevents them from altering the terms and tells them the bottom line has been reached.

- The buyer does a deal, then passes you on to someone else to lower your aspirations.

  Again be aware of the motive behind this move. Discuss and question the tactic. Always check first to make sure the person you're dealing with is a decision-maker.

- Final approval, says the buyer, is in the hands of someone who happens to be away at the moment. When this 'missing executive' returns they may want further concessions and lower still further your aspirations as to what you hoped you had achieved out of the deal.

  The best counter to this tactic is to put a time limit on the signing of the agreement. Talk to other people about the possible options.

- The scene's one familiar to TV police dramas – you find yourself dealing with a good guy and a bad guy at the sales interview.

  First the bad guy beats you down, then the good guy steps in sympathetically and you settle with him – less than you wanted but at least more than the bad guy would've given you.

- 'Take it or leave it' is something a professional salesperson would never say, but sometimes a buyer will say it, phrased differently.

  This is best met by justifying the situation, telling the buyer you would like to take them up on their offer, but it's not possible. Then come up with a counter-proposal and offer an alternative.

- The buyer wants 'little extras'.

  Don't be tempted just to *give* – remember what you've been taught and *trade*. You can also counter by telling the buyer salespeople in your company don't have authority to give extras. You can publish a list of extras available – without sacrificing any profit.

- Buyers will often ask for something they don't want to lower your aspiration or let you take it back later in exchange for another concession.

Counter by reducing the value to you of the concession they are making.

- The buyer attempts to probe your price structure – usually preceded by 'What if . . . ?' This must be countered effectively.

  Be wary of giving a price breakdown and cut down on the options available without going into too much detail. Stress that payment on receipt is good for your company.

Steps in negotiation
Research and preparation
The first step in any form of negotiation is research and preparation. A skilful negotiator will look at it from the other person's side as well as their own right from the very beginning.

All negotiation involves change. At the beginning of this section in the definition of negotiation, we made the assumption there was a proposal already on the table. We now therefore have to predict what could change as a result of the negotiation process.

Let's consider what we would like to get out of the negotiation – in other words, our objectives. For you, as a salesperson, the one presenting the proposal for the other side to consider, the ideal outcome would be for your proposal to be accepted as it stands, without negotiation. But your proposal might not necessarily represent the best possible outcome for you.

As a simple example, you could be offering 10 packs of your product at list price. You could be better off, however, and so could the customer, if it ended up with 20 packs at a lower price. Negotiation in this case resulted in change with a 'win-win' outcome. But it would not be a win for you if you lowered the price too much or not a win for the buyer if it took them much longer to use up the 20 packs.

Value is again the magic word. Both the methodical and creative sides to research are to

- discover all the things that could possibly change as a result of a negotiation and

- place a value and a cost on each one of them – for both sides.

We can illustrate this simply (see Figure 10). The key in placing a value and cost to you is *judgement* together with, of course, a complete familiarity with company policies and resources.

Judgement and *empathy* are the keys in placing a value and cost to the buyer.

	YOU	THEM
	[1]Value	Cost
ITEM	[2]Cost	Value
	[3]Value	Value
	[4]Cost	Cost

1. You might want a larger order, but that might take up extra storage space for the buyer's company – value to you and cost to them.
2. The buyer might want to stagger deliveries, which is going to cost you more for distribution.
3. You might decide to put the product on display and so might the buyer's company, which is of value to both sides.
4. A situation where it is of cost to both sides is, for example, if you grant them a discount at no profit and they over-order.

Fig. 10. Value.

There's really no excuse for you not getting it right on your side. And although you won't often get it completely right from the buyer's point of view, the nearer you get, the better prepared you'll be. To help you judge values, a good tip is to put each item in the category of a 'must' or a 'want' – again looking at things both from the point of view of your side and theirs. Another option is to give them a score on the scale of one to ten – again from the point of view of both sides.

Any item that's subject to change or likely to be introduced into the negotiation can be terms as *variable*. In the research and preparation stage the golden rule is to research methodically and creatively for variables.

Another key word is *package*. The hypothetical proposal on the table we can term the *original package*. What we finish up with at the end of the negotiations is the *eventual package* – possibly very different from the first one, but hopefully emerging as a 'win-win' situation.

Another key part of research and preparation is the forecasting and valuing of different possible eventual packages. Although the actual final package may well differ from any of the eventual packages you envisaged, the exercise has been of value in providing you during the cut and thrust of negotiation with mental yardsticks against which to measure any concessions you or the buyer might give.

Planning a strategy
Having researched, valued and packaged, you're now in a position to plan a strategy. For this you'll need to work out how you're going to open the negotiations, what questions you're going to ask and the concessions you plan to trade and for what on their side. Also to be taken into consideration are possible visuals you'll use and when, any new information by ways of benefits you have to give, how you're going to handle predictable objections and what sales material or samples you plan to leave. Most important, too, when and how to close.

Remember you can never be over-prepared. The more ready you are, the more flexible you can be, if necessary, in adapting your strategy. Knowing you've anticipated all the buyer's possible demands and considered how to meet them, you'll also be coolly confident.

Opening the negotiation
This also needs careful planning. The key is:

- How well do you know the other side?
- What kind of personality is their buyer/negotiator?
- What will their attitude be to your proposal?
- What will be their opening gambit?

If the buyer opens up first in a positive manner, look upon it as a buying signal and aim for a close. Negative openings by the other side must be devalued at once. Claims your competitors are considerably cheaper, for example, can be answered with a counterclaim to the effect that it's because they can't compete with the quality of your product or service.

Positive demands from the buyer deserve reward. If they tell you they're interested and will certainly go ahead if you could improve the terms a little, tell them how delighted you are and that you have some ideas you're sure will clinch it. Avoid committing yourself to making concessions in the initial stages, however, when a buyer opens up by saying there's not much point in even talking about it unless you're prepared to give them an extra discount. Tell them you're certain they'll be pleased with the package if they preserve an open mind about it.

If you judge a buyer's opening negative statement reveals hidden worries, such as fear of making a big decision or indeed any decision at all, or pressure from higher up, reassure them. The best way of doing this is with the 'four Fs', telling them you understand how they *feel*, that other people have *felt* the same way until they *found* that the *final* results more than lived up to their expectations, etc.

When you have the chance to open first, there are a number of possible alternatives, including:

- *Assumption*   In which you tell the buyer you're sure they'll agree the proposal as it stands will be of great benefit to them.
- *The positive approach*   You stress the need to reach agreement at once because of factors such as an imminent price increase, possible delivery delays, stock shortage, etc.
- *Exceptional value*   You 'confess' to the buyer you really shouldn't have proposed so good a package for them, but if they're keen to go ahead you're sure you'll be able to fix it.
- *Planned concession*   You've been giving the proposal some thought and you're keen to put a few ideas to the buyer which will make the offer even more attractive for them.

One thing you must **not** do at the beginning of any negotiation where you are the 'seller' is to come over in any way as the 'poor man at the rich man's gate'. Buyers when negotiating love to adopt a 'take it or leave it' attitude when they believe you are desperate to sell to them – no matter what the price.

The discussion phase
This follows the initial sparring in the opening phase. It's the stage where information is exchanged without commitment on either side. Interests are explored and assumptions tested. Follow these rules and you won't go wrong:

- Don't make any definite commitments.
- Get everything the other side have on their 'shopping list'.
- Don't let any particular point or issue bring about deadlock.

If the buyer attempts to force a concession out of you by pretending it's the only thing standing in the way between you and agreement, don't be tempted to comply. If you give anything away at this stage, the buyer will most likely make another demand, perhaps on the price. Once you've started backing down, it's very difficult to stop.

The best response is to divert the discussion away from the buyer's demand by opening up discussion on one of your planned variables without making or asking for any commitment. This is the art of the discussion phase, because by drawing the buyer out you're able to judge how they regard any ideas you suggest from the values and costs angle.

Good diversionary phrases include:

- 'We might be able to help you there . . .'
- 'I'll certainly make a note of that . . .'
- 'We certainly can be flexible on that point . . .'
- 'I'll have to have a word back at head office, but I'm sure it will be OK . . .'

Note that all these phrases are in the future tense. Any buyer worth their salt will certainly be trying to pin you down, but there are certain ways in which they'll reveal they're only testing the water, and testing you. Listen and watch for key signals such as:

- 'I doubt if we'll be able to . . .'
- 'The only major obstacle I can see . . .'
- 'At this point in time . . .'
- 'As things stand . . .'

If the buyer does signals like this, acknowledge it with a diversionary phrase, then side-step by either bringing in a variable into the discussion or asking a question.

Before you start proposing anything, the important thing is to satisfy yourself fully you have uncovered all the buyer's demands and concerns – the full 'shopping list', in fact. For example, you could find out that the buyer wants a lower price, *plus* free stock *and* follow-up support; but would be prepared to consider new lines *and* buying in quantity, *and* commit to some form of target.

Remember, too, that a 'win-win' outcome is what you're aiming for. It's to the buyer's benefit as well as yours you find out everything on their mind, so that as you reach the proposing phase, you can bargain one concession against another and end up with a package that's of maximum mutual value.

The proposing phase
This is usually triggered off by the phrase 'What if . . . ?' Definite commitments aren't being made, but firm suggestions are. You could, for example, be mentioning a possible extra discount in return for the buyer's company ceasing to do business with one of your competitors. This is the phase where you start working towards the stage where you can repackage the proposal.

Bargaining and agreement
This is the stage at which you start using the key words 'If . . . , then . . .' Now you're looking for agreement on all the details. This is where trading off concessions begins. Every concession you offer is conditional to you receiving one in return – where if the buyer agrees

to take an extra range of goods, for instance, you agree to the promotion they're asking for on a particular product.

Repackaging

This is the stage where you're re-presenting the original proposal but possibly in a very different form following changes brought about by concessions and the introduction of variables. However, the proposal should be of at least the original value to you and in addition be regarded as of greater value to the other side as well.

There could be details to be agreed, some further concessions to be traded and hard bargaining still to be done, but both sides should by now have a clear idea of what each wants. It's important in verbal exchanges to record what was decided – so as each point is agreed, *write it down*.

The summary

The summary is a vital phase in the negotiation. Its objectives are:

* *Administration*   detailed changes from the original proposal having been agreed, it's important there should be no misunderstanding.

* *Satisfaction*   It's your last opportunity to ensure the buyer's side are satisfied with the outcome from the aspect of *value*.

Now go through everything and read out all the details that have been agreed (*in the buyer's terms without mentioning the advantages to you!*), spelling out the concessions you have agreed in *benefit terms to the buyer*.

How you ensure the buyer's satisfaction with the value will depend on the person themselves and on what has occurred during the negotiation. But a little psychological persuasion will help. Develop your own repertoire of useful phrases like:

* 'Don't tell your competitors or they'll want the same sort of deal.'

* 'I'll have to make sure the boss is in a good mood when I tell him I've agreed to . . .'

* 'You drive a hard bargain. I'm not so sure I should have agreed to all this.'

Hackneyed, yes, but it will stand you in good stead when next you are confronted with the same individual!

TO SUM UP

Selling comes before negotiation. Both buyers and sellers need to develop the skills of selling and negotiation as responsibility for profits is passed down the line. Both have become poor men at the rich man's gate. However, a successful sales technique is not negotiation itself but laying the foundation on which negotiation can take place: to be a successful negotiator you must first develop your sales skills.

Negotiating is looked upon by many salespeople as thinking on your feet, but the fact of the matter is that 90% of the success of any good negotiator lies in the research, planning, anticipating (empathy with the customer) and preparation done before the meeting. Some see it as a trial of will, not of skill, but the truth of the matter is negotiating shouldn't be regarded as any sort of trial if the two sides are actively engaged in two-way communication and seeking a 'win-win' result.

Guard against thinking like the paranoid salesperson who sees successful negotiations as getting away with whatever they can from a buyer whom they're convinced would kick them out as soon as look at them! This sort of attitude means they're beaten before they start. Their grovelling or conniving puts them on unequal terms and leaves them trying to give away as little as possible.

> A good salesperson never gives anything away and a good negotiator always trades to the mutual benefit of both parties.

10

Achieving Aims, Closing the Sale and the Service Call

ACHIEVING AIMS OR CLOSING THE SALE

Everything we've talked about up to now has been leading us to the point where we can now concentrate on achieving our aims and getting the right decision from buyers. Everything taken on board so far would be wasted unless one learns to recognise closing signals. Ignore them at your peril.

Why are salespeople reluctant to ask for the order when it comes to the actual crunch? It's probably because they're frightened the prospective customer will say 'no'. They are aware a refusal could have a detrimental effect on their ego, confidence, self-esteem and respect. The fear of rejection is a very real one, but it's something that everyone faces in all spheres of life.

A salesperson should be trying to close or actively working towards doing so right from the start of the sales interview.

WHAT IS CLOSING?

Closing is the logical and natural conclusion to a sales presentation. It's a means of getting the buyer to make a decision favourable to your company. Sometimes it's no more than the salesperson making an appointment for a follow-up call.

Most people are not good at making decisions and many of them dislike spending money, particularly that of their company for which they have special responsibility. So you will find that, although a buyer is in a decision-making situation, they probably hate making a decision and are careful about spending money. A skilled salesperson, however, can dispel the uncertainty and help the buyer to come to a decision.

RULES FOR CLOSING

Closing at the right moment in the discussion is up to you, not the buyer, so you must always make sure you're the one to call the shots. Keep the aims of your call clearly in mind and anticipate likely closing signals, while thinking about the closes you may be able to employ.

Listen as well as watch for closing signals. Remember a closing signal is something the prospective buyer says, does or sometimes even writes which shows you they are moving towards a decision in your favour.

If the signals are strong enough, don't shy away from closing too early. The modified aim of an order can be made at any point in the selling process. While a closing signal gives you the opportunity to close, whether you take advantage of this will depend on how you size up the situation and how strong you judge the actual signal to be. As a good salesperson, you will develop empathy to the extent where you will sense it's the right moment to close on a decision.

WHEN TO CLOSE

Very often a sales presentation is perfect and professional, but fails to secure orders. When it came to it, the salesperson didn't ask for the order – they never closed the sale. Closing in the sales sense should become second nature to the salesperson – just like ending a conversation with someone. So:

- Be ready to close from the moment the meeting begins.
- Try to close all the time.
- Close the sale at the earliest possible moment.
- Close when the buyer signals they're ready to place the order.
- Close when nothing else remains to be done.

Don't forget – be alert for closing signals – those all-important indications from the buyer.

THE PSYCHOLOGY OF THE CLOSE

It's been said that the decision to make a decision is the most difficult decision to make. And the second most difficult decision is the decision to change in any way.

Just to keep on talking about your product or service and hope a prospect will suddenly make a decision without any prompting is optimistic. It's being doubly optimistic also to expect the buyer to come to a decision involving a *change* from that they are currently using.

But why not at least persuade the buyer by at least asking them do they want any of your product?

Well, the difficulty now is we've made it easier for the buyer to say 'no' and not change. Why not, however, make things really easy for the buyer and, at the least sign of genuine interest from them in your product, *make the decision for them*? If, for example, the prospective buyer comments the proposal sounds promising, tell them you're delighted they like it. So pleased are you, in fact, you'll arrange for delivery of a small quantity of the product, adding they can always ring you if they need more!

What you've done is to use psychology to turn the situation to your advantage. For if the prospect wants to get out of it, they're now a little on the spot – they are faced with making a definite decision to say 'no'. Your obvious confidence and assuming manner are making this very difficult for them.

No one would deny that closing the sale is the crucial important stage in every sales call. No matter how eloquent you are, if you can't close, you can't sell. Even if you do nothing else except ask for the order outright, you're on the way to becoming a salesperson and further ahead than those who can make an impressive presentation, but can't ask for the order.

Remember, that 80% of the time it's the salesperson who has to ask for the order – and customers expect to be asked for it.

If you were to ask a group of salespeople why they don't ask for the order, each one would probably give you a different answer. It would be by way of justification, a rationalisation of why they're reluctant to do so, ranging from 'On most occasions I don't think the prospect's ready for it' to 'If the presentation's going OK, it's likely to spoil things'. The true hidden answer is *fear* – fear of rejection.

But what's the most drastic thing that could happen because you tried to close? The customer won't shoot you, hit you – they won't even hate you. The worst that could happen is that they'll say 'no'. So just remember this: a salesperson doesn't start really selling until they get a 'no' for an answer.

How do you get over this irrational fear of rejection? Well, by adopting the principle of being tough minded. This does not mean being overbearing, blustering, browbeating or shouting down the prospective customer. It means devoting oneself to the seller's 'three Ds':

DEDICATION

DISCIPLINE

DETERMINATION

Dedication
Dedication means a belief in yourself, your company, the product and your profession as a salesperson.

Discipline
Discipline is training yourself by setting personal goals and being prepared to sacrifice time and effort to achieve them; it's about studying your product or service thoroughly and preparing to do the best for your clients and their needs.

Determination
Determination means a firm resolve to believe that 'no' is only the answer for now – not for ever; you will keep going with that presentation until the answer becomes 'yes'. 'No' will always be unacceptable and the sale worked for until it is won. If necessary, you will close more than once.

Don't think 'Can I have your order?' is the only close. There are many alternatives, some of which you will adopt as your own individual style. One general rule to go by, however, is this:

- To close, the salesperson is the one who must *ask* the closing question.

TRIAL CLOSES

The trial close is an attempt to close without risking a final 'no'. Experiment with these methods:

- Present the buyer with a choice – quantity, range, delivery, dates, for example.

- Take something for granted – such as when does the buyer want the goods delivered or, in the case of plant or machinery, who will be doing the installing?

- Ask questions seeking agreement on the buyer's part – 'Don't you think we'd better get down to assessing the quantities you'll need? We should go and see your production manager now, shouldn't we?'

- Make a physical move like taking out an order pad or a notebook – 'Let me just make a note of those quantities. May I use your phone to check up on delivery?' Then, standing up, 'If you could show me where they're to go . . .'

CLOSING STRONGLY

Trial closes don't always produce the desired result, however. Sometimes you've got to ask for the decision without beating about the bush. These techniques will help strengthen your closing:

- Summarise the buyer's agreements, but be careful they're what the buyer has agreed to rather than what you've said. It's vital not to remind them of what they didn't like.

- Recount a relevant case history to help a prospective buyer who cannot make up their mind.

- Turn any final objection to your advantage – 'So that's the only thing now which is worrying you, is it?'

- Offer any genuine inducement that will help.

- Mention holidays, extended delivery, delays generally, limited offers, price increases and so on to give the buyer a sense of urgency.

- Where there are alternatives in the way of style or performance always offer them.

- Use direct and positive assumption – 'Right, that's fine. So we'll book delivery to you early next month then.'

THE FINAL CLOSE

Look for the physical signals and listen for the verbal ones which tell you when the customer is ready to answer the final closing question.
    Verbal signals will be in the nature of such questions from the customer as:

- 'How can I pay for this . . . ?'
- 'What's the procedure for ordering . . . ?'

What they're saying in effect is

- 'I'm now ready to buy . . . ?'

The easiest physical signal to recognise is when the customer takes out a pen or cheque book. A smile, sitting forward in the chair or suddenly relaxing from a hitherto formal pose are equally good signals.

Having covered closing the sale in general terms, let's look at some ideas and tips from various sources which are based on actual experience of salespeople in the field. Some salespeople have an innate sense of timing. They know instinctively the right time to ask for an order. Most of us, however, have to learn and develop this sense of timing.

CLOSING THE SALE: SOME TIPS

1. One of the most common mistakes is to continue your presentation *after* the prospect has decided to buy. This is a killer. Many salespeople sell the buyer on the product or service, then 'unsell' them by continuing to rabbit on.

2. Always presume your prospect wants to buy; in fact act as if you take it for granted. Never say 'If you buy . . .' but 'When you buy . . .' Bring the subject of delivery or starting dates into the conversation. If you're not questioned by the buyer, it's almost a cert you'll get an order.

3. Once a prospective buyer says 'no', it's a real uphill struggle getting them to change their mind and say 'yes'. The buyer will feel they're losing face and no one likes doing that. So, if you can't get the buyer to say 'yes', don't provoke them into a downright refusal. Use the softly, softly approach and hope the moment will arrive when the buyer is ready to say 'yes'. You've just got to be patient and leave the door open.

4. Remember what you've already been told – watch and listen for buying signals from the prospect. As we've seen, these can come in questions, such as 'Do you think the delivery timescale is right for our business?' or hard statements like 'It looks just right for us'. It doesn't matter whether buying signals come after five minutes or well into the meeting – act immediately. Answer the buyer's question, then ask for the order.

5. When you do so, always give the prospective buyer a choice. Ask

when exactly they would like delivery, for instance, or query their colour preference. Again be positive – never say 'if' but 'when' and 'which'. By doing this you're allowing the prospect to make a minor decision which commits them before they actually agree to the main deal.

Although all salespeople use the same principles when selling, individual sales techniques will, of course, differ depending upon the personality of the seller and their particular product or service on offer. salespeople selling direct out of necessity tend to adopt a more 'hard-nosed' aggressive approach. They usually miss out or make a sale during the first interview, for they might not have the opportunity to make a second call. Representatives of manufacturing companies or industrial salespeople, however, make regular weekly or monthly calls. They have time to prepare the way for future selling visits and can afford to leave without asking for a final decision.

Arguments and controversy

Whatever your approach, never, never let yourself become involved in any argument or controversy – bite your tongue even if you know the statements made by a buyer are totally untrue. Once you start arguing you can expect the sales interview to close abruptly and to kiss goodbye to making the sale.

An argument could mean you've reached the point of no return, with no opportunity for a second chance. You've probably opened the door for a competitor for whom you have stupidly eased the way. Be tactful. Don't tell the prospect they're wrong without pulling any punches, but temper your reply along the lines of:

- 'Yes. Other people have thought exactly the same thing until I was able to show them the actual cost figures.'

By backing up your statement with some documentary evidence, you'll show the prospect they weren't alone in their opinion and will have avoided a head-on confrontation. You'll find most people will listen to reason if you treat them and their opinions tactfully.

Preconceived ideas

Equally, don't approach any prospective buyer with any preconceived notions based on the verdicts of others, particularly if you feel you're going to dislike them right from the start. Always look for the good points in others, not the bad ones. And don't moan or react angrily if the prospect fails to come across with an order. Too many sales-people are apt to become resentful if they fail to get an order. Any such demonstration on your part will only confirm to the prospect they were right to refuse you. To quote Scarlet O'Hara, 'tomorrow is another day' – there'll be other opportunities if you leave the buyer on amicable terms and have developed some form of rapport.

Objections

Remember, too, what we've already discussed regarding objections. Always turn them to your advantage with a comment like:

- 'I'm pleased you've mentioned that. It's a very fair point, but if you consider . . .'

In this way you can overcome an objection without the customer really knowing it. This is the subtle art of the really professional sales-person coming into play. You'll find you get a real kick out of the sense of achievement it gives you.

When closing do avoid using 'purchase' or 'buy'. People associate these words with spending and they could cause doubts in the mind of the prospective buyer.

Go over very interview afterwards and make an honest and can-did note of all the things that were said. Analyse the meeting and find out just when and why you won – or lost – that particular order.

EXAMPLES OF CLOSING THE SALE

'Direct' close

Although this is the most logical close of all, it's perhaps the least used because, as we've seen, so many salespeople fear 'no' and a rejection. We know, too, that some orders are lost due to weak pre-sentation rather than a weak close. So if the presentation has brought the buyer fully to the 'commit' apex of the selling process in Figure 9, then the direct, or 'ask for it', close will invariably succeed.

Even if you have an instinctive reluctance to use this close, don't shy away from asking for the order or a commitment, because you'll get a 'yes' far more frequently than you think. Even if the answer is 'no', this needn't mark the end of the sales interview. It merely means there's a reason for this and there's an objection which will give you an opportunity to resell, then to close again.

'Alternative' close

This is a frequently used close to get the prospect to make a decision of a secondary nature to achieve a salesperson's primary objective. We've covered one of the most obvious examples in the section on making telephone appointments. Instead of asking, 'Can I come and see you?', you offer the prospect a choice of times with 'Which will suit you best, Monday morning or Thursday afternoon?' Similar choices can be offered regarding delivery timings or methods of delivery, such as road or rail.

'Final objection'

A final objection may be the result of the clarification or handling of an earlier objection raised, by the salesperson isolating an objection, or by the buyer raising an objection as the result of the final close.

Once a final objection has been established and you realise the objection can be overcome, your response should be:

* 'So what you're saying is that apart from . . . you'd be happy to go ahead. Isn't that so?'

When the prospect answers 'Yes, subject to . . .' your answer, as the seller, is to overcome the objection and the sale is closed.

'Assumption'

This is where you assume right from the start the proposition is acceptable to the buyer. This can be done in several ways. One example is, at the end of the presentation, not to ask the buyer's permission to submit a quotation but tell them when to expect one. It's very unlikely for a buyer to object.

Assumption closes are often employed when products are being sold on a repeat-order basis, where the salesperson assumes the order level will allow their customer's stock to return to its usual level. If you're selling consumer, consumer durable or industrial repeat products, don't feel you have to justify each part of the order. By doing so you'll unnecessarily protract the proceedings.

'Summary'

Providing you have been asking a series of trial questions, you can start by summarising the customer's needs and then summarise the points of agreement you have established by trial closing while discussing benefits. Follow this by a simple question, such as 'Shall we go ahead then?', to complete this very effective closing technique.

The following two closes are particularly recommended when the customer is either inexperienced or loath to make decisions:

'Lost sale'

Frequently, after you've made a good presentation, you may find yourself confronted by a buyer with a totally negative attitude, who refuses to proceed any further. Now is not the time just to pick up your briefcase and leave wondering what lost you the sale. It's worth a try asking the buyer why you failed to convince them, stressing it would be a great help in the future if they told you just where you went wrong. The buyer can only do one of two things: be non-committal or (as you hope they will) bring to light the true objection, which you might well be able to overcome to conclude the sale successfully.

'Impending event'

Price rises, material shortages, industrial disputes, holidays, peak demands – events likely to happen in the near future can be cited as reasons why a customer should grant you an order now. Pressured by the thought of having to pay more, sustain delivery delays or miss out in any way, the inexperienced buyer is likely to give you a favourable decision.

'Step by step'

This consists of a series of easily answered indirect or alternative questions leading up to the final close. Typical examples are 'If you were to go ahead and buy . . . where would you like it delivered?' followed by 'And if you decided to do this, how would you like to pay, by cash or cheque?' Finally comes a simple 'So shall we do that then?'

'Major to minor'

Two questions are asked together, without a pause. The most important one is first: 'Would you like to buy . . . and, by the way, when would you like delivery?'

'Third party'

Relating the story of another satisfied customer works, but ensure all the parallels are relevant, i.e. that your buyer's business is of similar type and size:

- 'Your position is very much like that of ABC Company, who . . ., so shall we do the same for you?'

'Balance sheet'

• I like seeing the fors and againsts down on paper. It makes it easier to make important decisions, don't you think?'

'Bargain' close

You make a bargain with the customer from which both of you will benefit: 'If you can order now, I'll do . . .'

There are many other ways of closing in use today, including the 'fear close' and the 'dejection close', but you'll find these top 12 will cover nearly all situations and circumstances. There's no easy way to become overnight an expert on closing. Practice is the key, so make up your mind today to take one of the alternative closes and use it on every presentation for the next month until you're word perfect. Then move on to one of the others and so on until you're completely at home with each and every one of them. Take the time and make the effort to be a better closer. Don't postpone closing because you're afraid of failure or of rejection. A sales call is all about getting business.

THE SERVICE CALL

The service call is the one you make on a prospective buyer after you've converted them into a customer. Some salespeople refer to this as a 'courtesy' call, but there's more to it than that. It's dangerous to think of this most important call in those terms, as it implies all you have to do is bid your customer 'good day', ask them if there's anything they want, leave another business card and more sales literature and go cheerily on your way.

Every call you ever make, whether on a prospective buyer or an established customer, is made for one reason, and one reason only – to obtain business for your company. And the service call is no different.

Pause and ask yourself these questions before you make the call:

• Are you getting the maximum amount of business you can from the customer you're about to see?

• Are you competitors also doing business with this customer and if so, why?

• Are you confident that, despite competition, the customer will remain loyal to you?

- Are you sure you're seeing the right person – could there be others with whom you could be discussing business to better advantage?

- Have you asked the customer about their future short, medium or long-term plans – the one sure way to keep your product in mind?

Finally, and most important:

- Are you sure the customer adequately repays the amount of attention and the regular calls you make on them?

- Have you really looked into the *true potential* of this particular account?

Let's face it. There are only a limited number of ways open to you to increase your share of the market. To:

- Go prospecting and develop new business, by which you will set out to get as much of your competitors' business as you can.

- Increase business with your existing customers, which means your competitors will endeavour to obtain as much of your customers' business as they can. To safeguard this doesn't happen, take your service calls seriously and give each customer the good service to which they are entitled.

TO SUM UP

- Never expect a customer to hand you an order on a plate.

- Always ask for the order.

- Never assume it's easy for a customer to make a decision *to change*. You have to put in a lot of work to make it more difficult for them *not to change*.

- Put your close into action when the customer is showing interest – it makes it easier for them to say 'yes' and more difficult to say 'no'.

- If you can, save the customer the trouble of making any decision at all by your strong assumptions.

A salesperson does not really start selling until they get 'no' for an answer. Remember the 'three Ds': dedication, discipline and determination. Try different methods of closing and bear in mind a trial close does not always bring about the desired result. Salespeople generally have to ask for an order – most customers expect to be asked to order. Look for physical signs and listen for verbal clues the customer is ready to close.

Practise alternative closing strategies so you are competent in them all. Do not be afraid of failure or rejection: remember, a sales call is all about getting business. Take service calls seriously – they are not courtesy calls but a means of maintaining and establishing business.

11

Succeeding in Your Career

You've chosen selling as your career because you feel it's a worth-while job to be in – one that offers success, the happiness that results from being successful in a job and, most important, an inner sense of self-fulfilment. But, however professional and successful you become, you cannot afford to sit back complacently at any stage in your career and believe you've done it all. There will always be another challenge awaiting you.

You have to pay attention to your career if it is to continue pro-gressing and developing. In many ways it's rather like a car. By mak-ing sure your company or private vehicle is regularly serviced and cleaned, and checking tyre pressures, oil and radiator levels, you know it will get you to whatever destination you wish. Similarly, your sell-ing career will carry you to success, providing you keep upgrading your sales techniques, constantly strive to develop your professional-ism still further and maintain the right, positive attitudes.

SUCCEEDING IN YOUR JOB

Every company that employs you will reward you according to the effort and work you put in. Redundancy apart, it's been estimated that some 94% of people who otherwise lose their jobs are given their cards because of attitudes and not lack of skill. And attitudes are the reason, too, why between 80 and 90% of people are passed over for promotion.

Employers tend to classify salespeople as one of three basic types:

- One with the ability and keenness to do the job. This person is worth their weight in gold. They'll be successful anyway with or without the assistance of others. But with the right sort of help, they can reach the top of the ladder quicker.
- A person who is keen but short on ability. As long as the person is keen, they can be easily taught selling techniques. They, too, can achieve success through selling and, by applying themselves, often reach the top.
- A person with ability, but very little desire and ambition. They

know how to sell, and can do it, but for some reason known best to themselves put up a mental barrier between them and success. 'Well, it's a job . . .' is an attitude commonly found.

Experience among sales directors and other senior managers shows that any effort put into trying to develop and change the attitude of the last salesperson above is just not worth it. Why bother when one can employ people of the first two categories? Attitude in your job, as in everyday life, is the most important aid to getting on.

THE RIGHT ATTITUDES

Be friendly
Friendliness is a way of reaching out to people. It's the ability to go beyond the bounds of common courtesy. It may require some effort on your part, if you're not a naturally outgoing person, but then the habit of doing things for other people always did need extra effort.

Pay attention
By being attentive and listening to the other person's side, you can pay attention to their strengths, weaknesses and to their needs.

Be helpful
However busy successful people are, they always find time to help others. There'll be many times when you'll be helped by others. The great thing about selling is it gives you many opportunities, too, to help people, including your colleagues in the office. By helping people get what they want from life, you'll get what you yourself want.

Be tactful
Tact is seeing things from another person's point of view and respecting their sensitivity. It's being able to empathise with them. The road to hell is paved with good intentions and many remarks are probably meant to be friendly, but they're said carelessly with the wrong sort of tone. Never put the other person down, even if it's intended as a joke. Bear in mind you probably exhibit some idiosyncrasies or behave in a way puzzling to those you meet, so respect the same in others!

Show enthusiasm
Enthusiasm's catching, so let people see how enthusiastic you are. Everybody likes an enthusiastic person. You'll not only feel bright

within yourself, but you'll have an uplifting influence on the mental attitude of the other members of your sales team.

OTHER CONSIDERATIONS

- Do more than what you're paid to do. Give the job all your best shots. You can then walk tall and hold your head up high among colleagues and employers alike.

- Get to know and like the people with whom you work. As members of the sales team or the other departments in the company providing backup services, they're contributing to your success. Together you stand, divided you fall. Judge every one of them on their strengths, not weaknesses.

- Don't gossip. Like Chinese Whispers, facts are distorted, lost or, worse still, substituted by false ones. Gossip can destroy you and your colleagues. Speculation wastes time, is usually inaccurate and damages everyone taking part in it.

- No company is perfect – it's as strong or as weak as the people it employs and nobody is perfect. Don't let minor irritations annoy you. Recognise and accept them for what they are and rise above it all.

- Take everything in your stride, and that applies particularly to setbacks of any sort. Setbacks are failures only if you consider them as such. Look upon them more as providing opportunities for you to exercise your ingenuity. Feel confident within yourself. Believing you can win and having total belief in your personal ability will help you succeed.

- Defend your company against anyone who knocks it or its products. They're not just having a go at your company, they're in fact knocking you as well. You wouldn't be working for the company if it wasn't worth while, would you? It's providing jobs for the people who work for it, keeping the shareholders happy, is a part of the nation's commerce and industry, and has its own place in the community. OK, so it's got its faults, but they're down to you and anyone else who works there and makes up the company.

- Believe in your immediate boss and in the other senior executives. Someone has to take control of things and issue instructions, otherwise the company would be like a ship without officers on the bridge. The executives in your company got where they are because of their knowledge and experience of the game. If they weren't up to the job, they'd have been replaced to safeguard the company's survival, particularly in today's competitive commercial environment.

- As well as the senior executives, believe in the board of directors. Accept their policies and instructions in good faith and accept they are the right people to occupy those positions.
- Look out for promotion opportunities and prepare yourself to take advantage of them when they arise. Many companies these days promote from within and then it becomes a case of 'whom?' There's a real need for people ready to accept responsibility – so be prepared!

- Always look on the bright side of life. Be cheerful and think, act and talk positively. A smile is more profitable than a frown. If you do come across any negative thinkers in your company, avoid getting involved with them at all costs. A negative attitude can adversely infect others. You don't want them undermining your morale because you've got your sights set high on bigger things.

- Get involved with the successful people in your company, those with a good track record and position in the organisational structure. You can learn a lot by associating with successful people and some of that success can rub off on you. We are judged by the company we keep.

Keep selling ideas in selling situations. Be patient, if at first a customer doesn't accept an idea. There's a resistance to change in every one of us. If your idea's rejected, it might only need a little modifying before you're able to put it forward again.

12

Fourteen Maxims for Success

1. Of all the things you wear, your expression is the most important.
2. You never get a second chance to make a first impression.
3. You have two ears and one mouth – use them in proportion.
4. The only place where Success comes before Work is in the dictionary (Vidal Sassoon).
5. Asking a stupid question is better than correcting a stupid mistake.
6. Always plan the work and work the plan – no one plans to fail but many fail to plan.
7. A way to a person's money is through their door.
8. Nothing recedes like success and the only thing more infectious than enthusiasm is lack of it.
9. Customers are perishable, and no customer can be worse than no customer.
10. A good plan today is better than a great plan tomorrow.
11. Force is never as effective as leverage.
12. Every crowd has a silver lining (P.T. Barnum).
13. The bitterness of poor quality still remains long after the sweetness of low cost is forgotten.
14. Production minus sales is scrap.

Always remember: **fortune favours the courageous, but know which way the wind blows; by vigilant for change – do not unduly rock the boat, get on with your captain and prosper.**

Further Reading

STARTING A BUSINESS

How to Be an Entrepreneur, I Phillipson (Kogan Page, 1993).
Starting Up Your Own Business, 3i (Investors in Industry).
Starting Your Own Business – the Practical Steps (Department of Employment).
Starting a Business From Home, Graham Jones (How To Books, 4th edition 1999).
Starting a Small Business, Alan & Deborah Fowler (Warner Books).
Swim With the Sharks, Harvey McKay (Warner Books).
Working for Yourself, G Golzen (Kogan Page, 1995).
The Wyvern Business Library, Wyvern House, 7 The Business Park, Ely, Cambridgeshire CB7 4JW. Suppliers of a wide range of business books, available through mail order.

ORGANISING YOURSELF

Getting Things Done: The ABC of Time Management, Edwin C Biss (Warner Publications).
10-Minute Time and Stress Management, Dr David Lewis (Piatkus).

MARKETING & PROMOTION

Effective Negotiating, C Robinson (Kogan Page, 1995).
How to Do Your Own PR, Ian Phillipson (How To Books, 1995).
Making Direct Mail Work, Peter Arnold (How To Book, 1999).
Managing Your Sales Team, John Humphries (How To Books, 2nd edition, 1999).
The Secrets of Effective Direct Mail, John Fraser-Robinson (McGraw-Hill, London 1989).
The Secrets of Successful Copywriting, Patrick Quinn (Heinemann, London).
Seductive Selling, Kit Sadgrove (Kogan Press).
Total Confidence, Philippa Davies (Piatkus).

Writing to Sell, The Complete Guide to Copywriting for Business, Kit Sadgrove (Robert Gale, London 1991).

How to Plan Direct Mail, I Maitland (Cassell, 1995).

How to Sell a Service, Malcolm McDonald and John Leppart (Heinemann, 1986).

How to Win Customers, Heinz Goldman (Plan, London 1980).

Selling, P Allen (Pitman Publishing, 1991).

Selling to the Public Sector, Jim Green (How To Books, 2000).

Successful Marketing for the Small Business, Dave Patten (Kogan Page).

Successful Negotiation, R Maddox (Kogan Page, 1988).

Writing a Report, John Bowden (How To Books, 4th edition 1997).

Index